THE OPEN UNIVERSITY
Arts: A Third Level Course
Modern Art and Modernism:
Manet to Pollock

BLOCK II (Units 5–6)

Impressionism and Degas

Prepared by Nigel Blake, Charles Harrison and Di Norman,
with additional material supplied by
Francis Frascina, Aaron Scharf and Belinda Thomson.

The Open University Press

The Open University Press
Walton Hall,
Milton Keynes
MK7 6AA

First published 1983

Designed by the Graphic Design Group of the Open University.

Text set in 12/13½ pt Garamond Medium.

Printed in Great Britain by Linneys of Mansfield.

ISBN 0 335 11106 8

This text forms part of an Open University course. The complete list of units in the course appears at the end of this text.

For general availability of supporting material referred to in this text, please write to Open University Educational Enterprises Limited, 12 Cofferidge Close, Stony Stratford, Milton Keynes, MK11 1BY, Great Britain.

Further information on Open University courses may be obtained from the Admissions Office, The Open University, PO Box 48, Walton Hall, Milton Keynes, MK7 6AB.

1.1

Block II Impressionism and Degas

Contents

Set reading

George Heard Hamilton, *Painting and Sculpture in Europe 1880 – 1940,* Penguin Books, 1981.

Francis Frascina and Charles Harrison (eds), *Modern Art and Modernism: A Critical Anthology,* Harper and Row, 1982 (referred to as the Reader).

You should read the following texts from the Reader in the course of working through Block II.

8 J. -K. Huysmans, 'L'Exposition des Indépendants in 1880'
41 E. Lipton, 'The Laundress in Late Nineteenth Century French Culture'

You will also need to read the relevant extracts in the *Supplementary Documents*.

Broadcasting

The following programmes are broadcast while you are working on Block II.

Television programme 5   *Pissarro*
Television programme 6   *Van Gogh: rooted in the soil*
Radiovision programme 5   *The First Impressionist Exhibition*
Radiovision programme 6   *Pissarro and politics*

You should look at the notes and illustrations which accompany these programmes before the broadcasts.

The following broadcasts are also relevant to this block.

Television programme 2   *Artists' techniques*
Television programme 3   *Manet*
Television programme 4   *Monet*
Radiovision programme 3   *Baudelaire, imagination and modern life*
Radiovision programme 4   *Images of prostitution*
Radiovision programme 8   *Peasants*

List of illustrations associated with Block II

(These are provided in separate booklets. You should refer to the captions printed with the plates for full details of the pictures. Those marked with an asterisk are not referred to in the text but relate to the broadcasts.)

Colour plates

1 Monet, *La Grenouillère*
2 Renoir, *La Grenouillère*
3 Monet, *Railway Bridge at Argenteuil*
4 Monet, *Boulevard des Capucines*
5 Monet, *Autumn at Argenteuil*
6 Renoir, *Pont Neuf, Paris*
7 Renoir, *Monet Working in his Garden*
8 Pissarro, *Factory near Pontoise*
9 Monet, *Waterlilies*
10 Monet, *Impression. Sunrise*
11 Pissarro, *Coach at Louveciennes*
12 Pissarro, *Bourgeois House at L'Hermitage, Pontoise*

13 Degas, *The Absinthe Drinker*
14 Degas, *Café Concert*
15 Degas, *The Rehearsal of the Ballet on Stage* (oil)
16 Degas, *The Rehearsal of the Ballet on Stage* (pastel)
17 Degas, *Racehorses at Longchamps*
18 Degas, *Young Spartan Girls Provoking the Boys*
19 Degas, *Carriages at the Races*
20 Degas, *The Rehearsal*
21 Degas, *Women Sitting in Front of a Café*
22 Degas, *Women Ironing*
23 Pissarro, *Hoar Frost*
*24 Gervex, *Rolla*

Black-and-white plates

1 The Impressionists

Impressionism and Modernism

We have been concerned to point out in this course that works of art are best understood by reference to the historical conditions of their production. We also wish to stress the value of reading contemporary criticism as a guide to at least some aspects of these conditions. One important caution must be borne in mind, however: contemporary reactions are likely to emphasize what was novel, since it is the novel that is remarked and commented on, either favourably or unfavourably. Subsequent criticism may stress the same novel features since these are seen as just what make an artist or movement art-historically progressive. An avant-garde movement thus tends to be identified as such on the one hand in terms of the ways in which it appeared to break contemporary standards of taste and decorum, and on the other in terms of those further developments which it enabled in doing so. Within the Modernist tradition, the assumption tends to be made that these are one and the same; i.e. that the breaking of redundant rules is what makes development possible, indeed that this is what development in art actually means. But it need not be true that they are the same. Much of the outrage with which Manet's *Olympia* was greeted was attributable to the polite public's perception that the woman represented was an unabashed prostitute. Yet Modernist criticism and history has tended to stress that Manet's radicalism lay not so much in *what he represented* as in his *means of representing.* Even where attention is paid to sources of imagery, etc., as in Fried's writing, these are seen essentially as referents for a *way* of representing. Sources are still pretexts (for subjects themselves seen as pretexts). As we have seen, the Modernist tradition locates Manet at the forefront of a series of changes in 'surface', technique and so on, and suggests that it was his treatment that was found unacceptable. It is not generally claimed that Manet initiated a modern tradition of explicit nudes. Francis Frascina was concerned to redress this balance in the previous block, and to show that Modernism has tended to underestimate the significance of Manet's choice of subjects, and thus to disregard many of the more traditional aspects of his practice. T.J. Clark, in his article on *Olympia,* was similarly concerned to uncover from contemporary criticism what may have been left unsaid precisely because it was so widely felt.

The point I am trying to make is that if we pay attention only to what was seen as novel or 'unacceptable' by contemporary critics, or if our retrospective assessment is too much governed by modern preoccupations, we may lose sight of those features which were taken for granted, or seen as traditional or acceptable, and thus as undeserving of particular remark. We would thus be restricting our own enquiries within the framework handed down to us through a particular tradition of criticism and interpretation, in this case the Modernist tradition.

This caution is particularly relevant to the discussion of Impressionism and of its art-historical status as the first avant-garde movement. (Please note that while we use the label 'Impressionist' throughout this block, it was not first applied to the work of the typical members of the group – Claude Monet, Auguste Renoir, Alfred

Sisley and Camille Pissarro – until 1874.) The following passage written by the Italian critic and art historian Lionello Venturi in 1963 provides an example of how the status of Impressionism has been established within the Modernist tradition.

> The Impressionists took a different direction from the Realists, since, instead of trying to represent nature in its entirety, they selected one element – light – to be treated as an independent and organic element of style. . . . In its development Impressionist art depicted nature but retained an awareness of its distinction, its own abstraction from nature; for this reason modern art traces its origins back to Impressionism. . . . Rejection of subject – particularly the 'significant' subject – concentration on light, finishing of the unfinished, splitting up of colours, and an autonomous view of reality are all aspects of that revolution of taste which bears the name of 'Impressionism'.
>
> ('Impressionism', *Encyclopedia of Modern Art*, Vol. VII, Col 825-6, 1963)

Note that Impressionism is here discussed in terms of a break with 'the Realists'. We need to distinguish two different possible interpretations of realism: Realism (with a capital 'R'), for which Courbet, with his particular social and political aims and interests stands as exemplar, and realism as a philosophical position or approach to the world. Modernists tend to conflate the two, as Venturi does here.

The issue of whether Impressionism can be seen as a realistic art is crucial and one that will be developed during the block. Answers to this question may also help to determine our view of Degas' position in relation to the Impressionist movement.

'Realism' and Impressionism

First please remind yourself of the substance of the discussion of Courbet and representations of the nude in Block I (pages 10–16). Realism with a capital 'R' is normally used to refer to a dominant 'movement' in the figurative arts and in literature from about 1840–1870/80. It was strongest in France, but versions existed elsewhere on the continent, in England and the United States. As Linda Nochlin claims, 'Its aim was to give a truthful, objective and impartial representation of the real world, based on meticulous observation of contemporary life' (*Realism*, 1971, page 13). She goes on to discuss the historical and conceptual problems which arise from the notion of Realism, and you could profitably consult this book. However, for our purposes a more general discussion is needed here (in Block V the term 'realism' is more fully considered in the light of how changes in its meaning, and artistic traditions associated with it, are pertinent to Cubism).

Nochlin's definition, which is a paraphrase of the view of many mid-nineteenth century French writers and artists, could be used to describe the aim of Impressionism. And there is some historical justification for this. The critic and champion of Courbet's Realism, Jules-Antoine Castagnary (1830–1888) wrote in 1863 and 1868 of a development or change within 'Realism' in art. He did this in the light of changes in the notion of how 'realism' could be represented in painting. First I will quote him and then consider how his contemporary view helps us understand 'realism' as practised by Impressionists.

> The object of painting is to express, according to the nature of the means at its disposal, the society which produced it . . . Society is actually a moral being which does not know itself directly and which, in order to become conscious of reality, needs to externalize itself, as the philosophers say, to put its potentialities in action and to see itself in the general view of their products. Each era knows itself only through the deeds it has accomplished: political deeds, literary deeds, scientific deeds, industrial deeds, artistic deeds . . . As a result, painting is not at all

an abstract conception, elevated above history, a stranger to human vicissitudes, to the revolutions of ideas and customs; it is part of the social consciousness, a fragment of the mirror in which the generations each look at themselves in turn, and as such it must follow society step by step, in order to take note of its incessant transformations.

('Salon de 1863', quoted in Nochlin *Realism and Tradition in Art, 1848–1900, Sources and Documents,* 1966, page 64)

The word *naturalism,* which I use to define the tendencies of today, is not new in the history of art, and it is one of the reasons that makes it preferable to the word *realism.* Each time we encounter a nation, or, within a nation, a group of men taking the interpretation of surrounding life as the immediate object of painting, and striving to make a visual reproduction of society in its natural setting, that art has been, that art is – called naturalist . . . [Naturalism] says to the artist: Be free! Nature and life, which are the eternal raw materials of all poetry, Go, and come back to show other men what you have found there. You all live on the same clod of earth, at the same moment of time, and you are all the same thing. But *yours* is a deeper and clearer mirror, which perceives objects better; your art is a condenser that seizes and renders palpable the most fleeting sensations.

('Salon de 1868', quoted in Nochlin, *ibid,* pages 66–68)

Naturalism here becomes an offshoot of preoccupations associated with Realism, and it reflects what was a complicated and often confused interaction between 'naturalism' and 'realism'. Both were used to describe not only close observation but detailed 'reproduction' of natural objects. Many of the Impressionists' choices of subject matter accorded with Castagnary's 1863 view of urban idylls and forms of recreation; part of the social consciousness of a bourgeois culture. Their techniques were more in tune with his 1868 view of naturalism.

I am not suggesting that Castagnary was the theorist for Impressionism, but that his criticism helps us understand how notions of 'realism' and 'naturalism' overlapped, providing a critical discourse in which Impressionism developed as a practice. In fact you'll see from the Castagnary text in the *Supplementary Documents* that he saw in Impressionism two aspects; one rooted in tradition, according with his view of naturalism, the other 'subjective fantasies; a pretext for dreams' and 'without possible verification in reality'. It is the painters Pissarro, Monet, Sisley, Renoir and Morisot that he regards as following the former and thus the aim of realism/naturalism.

Meyer Schapiro is an example of a twentieth-century art historian who bases his interpretation of Impressionism on the sort of approach offered by Castagnary. He is as interested as Castagnary in the social and cultural determinants on such works of art.

Early Impressionism had a moral aspect. In its unconventionalized, unregulated vision, in its discovery of a constantly changing phenomenal outdoor world of which the shapes depended on the momentary position of the casual or mobile spectator, there was an implicit criticism of symbolic social and domestic formalities, or at least a norm opposed to these. It is remarkable how many pictures we have in early Impressionism of informal and spontaneous sociability, of breakfasts, picnics, promenades, boating trips, holidays and vacation travel. These urban idylls not only present the objective forms of bourgeois recreation in the 1860's and 1870's; they also reflect in the very choice of subjects and in the new aesthetic devices the conception of art as solely a field of individual enjoyment, without reference to ideas and motives, and they presuppose the cultivation of these pleasures as the highest field of freedom for an enlightened bourgeois detached from the official beliefs of his class. In enjoying realistic pictures of his surroundings as a spectacle of traffic and changing atmospheres, the cultivated rentier was experiencing in its phenomenal aspect that mobility of the environment, the market and of industry to which he owed his income and his freedom. And in the new Impressionist techniques which broke things up into finely discriminated points of color, as well as in the 'accidental' momentary vision, he found, in a degree hitherto unknown in art, conditions of sensibility closely related to those of the urban promenader and the refined consumer of luxury goods.

As the contexts of bourgeois sociability shifted from community, family and church to commercialized or privately improvised forms – the streets, the cafés and resorts – the resulting consciousness of individual freedom involved more and more an estrangement from older ties; and those imaginative members of the middle class who accepted the norms of freedom, but lacked the economic means to attain them, were spiritually torn by a sense of helpless isolation in an anonymous indifferent mass. By 1880 the enjoying individual becomes rare in Impressionist art; only the private spectacle of nature is left. And in neo-Impressionism, which restores and even monumentalizes the figures, the social group breaks up into isolated spectators, who do not communicate with each other, or consists of mechanically repeated dances submitted to a preordained movement with little spontaneity.

('The Nature of Abstract Art' (1937), in Schapiro, *Modern Art: 19th and 20th Centuries*, 1978)

Monet, Renoir, and the 'Impressionist project'

Now take out the two paintings by Monet and Renoir of *La Grenouillère* (**Col.pls II.1** and **II.2**) and keep them to hand. These two pictures were painted in the summer of 1869 while Monet (1840–1926) and Renoir (1841–1919) were working together at Croissy, six miles from Paris (see Block I, page 22, Figure 6). They had met while students at Gleyre's atelier (Television programme 2) in 1862, together with Frédéric Bazille (1841–71) and Sisley (1839–99). Renoir had had one painting, a portrait of Lise, accepted by the 1869 Salon. Monet's submission of that year was rejected entirely despite the success of some early seascapes in 1865, and he now wrote to a former patron, 'that fatal rejection has almost taken the bread out of my mouth; in spite of my not at all high prices, dealers and collectors turn their backs on me'. The series of small paintings which the two artists produced at La Grenouillère, a popular bathing place on the Seine, is normally seen as marking the beginning of Impressionism; marking that is to say, the moment at which the work of these two artists can be distinguished in some specific way from the mainstream of modern art at the time. (Another of Monet's paintings of La Grenouillère is discussed in detail in Television programme 5.)

In the light of the previous block you should by now have an idea of what 'Modern painting' might have meant in Paris in 1869. Some dates may help. *Olympia* had been exhibited at the Salon four years before. Delacroix had died six years before at the age of sixty-five, Ingres two years before at the age of eighty-seven. Of senior artists still working, Corot was seventy-three, Millet fifty-four and Courbet fifty. Monet's teacher Boudin (1824–98) had been painting small 'impressionistic' beach scenes for some years (**Pl.II.1**) and had gained support from Baudelaire. The Barbizon painters, Théodore Rousseau (1812–67), Virgilio Diaz de la Pena (1807–76), Constant Troyon (1810–65) and their close associate Charles Daubigny (1817–78), had for some time been painting and exhibiting landscapes and country scenes with much of their work done out of doors (see **Pls II.2, II.3**). Works by all of these might be seen at the Salon in the late 1850s and 1860s, though such conservative figures as Gérôme and Cabanel were exerting a strong influence over the jury in 1869 (**Pl.II.4**). Within the Salon, landscape painting may not have been accorded the status still reserved for history painting or the nude, but it had long been established as an acceptable genre. Rousseau had been among those whose work was featured in the Paris World's Fair of 1855, together with Ingres and Delacroix. Courbet's 'Pavillon du Réalisme' had no doubt attracted the attention of many younger artists at the same time, and both he and Manet had exhibited at the 1867

World's Fair, albeit outside the official areas. The Salon des Refusés of 1863, heterogeneous though it must have been, had helped to publicize the idea of dissent from the Salon, even if it did not permit identification of a distinctively modern art. Among those known to have shown were Manet, Whistler, Jongkind, Pissarro, Cézanne and Guillaumin.

Monet, Renoir, Bazille and Sisley had maintained close contact after the closing of Gleyre's atelier in 1864 and in the mid-1860s had painted together at Chailly near Barbizon. Diaz, Millet and Corot were all working in the same area during that time. The Barbizon painters and Corot, Courbet and Manet were those among whose works the younger artists tended to look for examples of modern practice in painting. By 1869 all those who were to be closely associated with the development of Impressionism were part of the circle of painters and writers who gathered around Manet at the Café Guerbois in Paris. Degas, Bazille, Renoir and Zola were then living in Paris and went there often. Pissarro, Monet, Sisley and Cézanne joined the company on their visits to the capital. The members of this informal gathering became known as the 'Batignolles group', after the area in which the café was located (see Block I, page 38 and **Pl.II.5**). Bazille's painting of his own studio (**Pl.II.6**) includes portraits of Manet, Monet, Edmond Maître (a friend of Renoir and Bazille), Renoir or Sisley and possibly Zola. The tall figure of Bazille himself was painted by Manet.

▶ In the summer of 1869 both Monet and Renoir were hard pressed to find enough money either for food or for paint. Look carefully now at the two paintings of La Grenouillère and consider the following questions.

1   What features are likely to have been seen as normal and conventional within the practice of modern painting at the time?

2   What features do they have in common which might serve to distinguish them from other modern paintings of the time?

3   What significant differences are there between them? (Don't spend too long considering this question. I ask it as a way to make you check your answers to Question 2, and not simply because I want you to distinguish Monet's style from Renoir's at this point.)

4   In the light of your answers to (1) and (2), what features might have struck a contemporary observer as particularly novel (one, say, who was familiar with the wide range of work shown in the Salon)? ◀

▷ 1   The *general type* of subject, people at leisure in the open air, was certainly unexceptional by this time, if not common, though as a subject for finished paintings it had only comparatively recently become independent from a literary or explicit moralizing content on the one hand, and from connections with group portraiture on the other hand. (There are beach scenes, for instance, in Boudin's work, but they tend to be sketches. Manet's *Déjeuner sur l'herbe* could still be seen as a picture of recognizable individuals.) The 'sketchy' treatment of both works was by no means unusual as such. As early as 1837, Théophile Gautier had complained that Daubigny's works showed 'merely spots of colour juxtaposed'. Nor was painting in the open air a novel practice in itself. Boudin had advocated it to Monet, and Couture and Gleyre had encouraged their students to work out of doors where appropriate as part of the preparatory work for finished compositions. In the Salon, if not in the Academy, 'a painterly touch' or 'experimental technique' could be appropriately demonstrated in several genres, landscape in particular. And a vocabulary of appreciation for such technical displays, for example in the works of Couture and Delacroix, was already well established in criticism before Manet became a notorious figure (see quotation from Boime, Block I, page 17).

The basic organization of the two compositions is also comparatively conventional, with vertical motifs (the trees at left and cabins at right) framing a group of figures in the middle distance, the boats providing a 'lead in' in the foreground, and the far bank and trees serving to enclose the space. Such strong light/dark contrasts may not have been common, but they could be found in some works of Corot and, as you saw in Block I, in recent paintings by Manet. (Such changes in technical procedure were discussed in 'Manet's training', Block I, pages 16–20. See also Television programme 2.)

2   Apart from obvious similarities of subject the paintings share a wide tonal range (from darkest dark, to lightest light) with occasional sharp contrasts of light and dark, combined with the use of bright and varied colour. Both painters have represented the play of light and reflection on the rippled surface of the water as a major feature in what they have observed. In both paintings the brushwork is clearly discernible as a sequence of strokes, dabs and touches. One way to put this would be to say that the functions of painting and colouring are pulled further apart than was normal from the purposes of drawing and delineation. We should remember that skill in the use of colour was less easily picked out by the prevailing critical vocabulary than evidence of skill in drawing; or, at least, that a painter's use of strong and bright colour tended to be remarked *as such,* rather than discussed in terms of its representational functions.

3   The brushwork of the Renoir is more broken and detailed, particularly in the middle distance and foreground, and the contrast of tone overall is less extreme than in the Monet. The sense of 'atmosphere' in the Renoir seems partly produced by the agitation of the brushwork. (He probably used finer and softer brushes than Monet.) In the Monet, 'atmosphere' seems to be defined rather in terms of a particular quality in the depicted light. You may feel that the two paintings were done at different times of day and under slightly different weather conditions, and that that accounts for some differences in appearances. But beware of making such assumptions. Even the most fluent and confident of painters would require several hours to paint a picture the size of these. They are more likely to have worked on the two paintings over several days. Where the artists' interest was in representing a scene under very particular conditions of light and weather, the problem was to develop a set of techniques which would *enable them to do so.* One important function of any representational technique must be to serve as a visual aide-mémoire – a means both to store visual (or other) impressions and to facilitate their recovery. There was no automatic solution to this problem. The appropriate techniques had to be worked out and practised. What we can say is that the two painters seem to have aimed to *represent* La Grenouillère under different light and weather conditions. And we might expect these differences to be related to differences in technical habits and skills.

A similar point can be made about the differences in composition. Renoir seems to have set his easel up closer to the central island than Monet. But he *need* not have done so. He may rather have made a different selection from within the *same* visual field, drawn by his interest in the figures and their costumes, where Monet was more engaged by the surface of water. It would be very generally true to say that Renoir's earlier work shows him to have been more concerned than Monet with the costumed human figure as a subject, and less concerned with particular qualities of light. The increasing identification of Monet as the central figure of Impressionism, from the later 1870s onwards, was largely the result of his overriding interest in the effects of changing light on outdoor surfaces.

4   In answering this question two different themes need to be considered *and related.* The first is subject matter, the second is technique. Or we might say *what* is represented, and *how* it is represented. Unless we're historians of costume and

fashion or social historians of a specialized cast of mind, we may miss one important characteristic in the subject of these pictures, and one which would have been instantly recognizable to contemporary spectators. These are neither picturesque country scenes, nor scenes of elegant aristocratic diversion, nor representations of the proletariat or peasantry at play, for each of which there existed a long line of art-historical precedents. These are scenes of *bourgeois* recreation, not in the landscape of the countryside, but in the outer *suburbs,* at a place which was neither fashionably genteel, nor fashionably picturesque, but which could be comfortably reached by rail from Paris for a day outing. (Incidentally, in contemporary French slang, *grenouille* was a term for a 'fast woman', a meaning which would escape most twentieth-century viewers.) Much later, in 1877, the critic Charles Bigot complained of the Impressionists, 'It's not real nature that they have looked at and tried to render, it's above all nature and the way one glimpses it in the city and its environs' (see **Col. pl. II. 3**, Monet, *The Railway Bridge at Argenteuil*).

A quotation from Monet's teacher Boudin serves to remind us

a   that such bourgeois and suburban subjects were not among those normally represented at the time;

b   that the possibility of a new 'modern' subject-matter was still a matter of interest in the circles of the early Impressionists;

c   that the socially realistic aspects of such interests had roots both in the work of Courbet and in Baudelaire's programme for a 'Painter of Modern Life'.

> The peasants had their painters . . . that is fine but, between ourselves, these middle-class people who are strolling on the jetty at the hour of sunset, have they no right to be fixed upon canvas, to be brought to our attention? Between us, they are often resting from strenuous work, these people who leave their offices and cubby holes. If there are a few parasites among them, are there not also people who have fulfilled their task? Here is a serious, irrefutable argument.
>
> (Boudin, letter to Martin, 3 September 1868, quoted in Rewald, *History of Impressionism,* 1961, page 44.)

Such ideas had certainly been raised by the work of Manet, but it was not until the early 1870s and after his contact with the younger Impressionists that Manet was to follow them in working out of doors on suburban scenes of bourgeois leisure (**Pl.II.7**). Although the subject of the *Déjeuner sur l'herbe* (1863) could be seen to evoke St Ouen or Argenteuil, both Parisian riverside suburbs (see Block I), its light is after all a *studio* light. Which leads us to considerations of technique. The saturation (purity) and intensity (brightness) of colour was certainly maintained in the La Grenouillère paintings beyond what was normally seen as acceptable even in modern painting. It is partly the combination of this brilliance of colour with an extreme tonal range which gives these paintings their distinctive appearance. In normal practice, even in modern circles, it would be assumed that the adoption of a wide tonal range would work *against* the intensification of colour. We can more easily discriminate between colours – indoors at least – where the lighting is comparatively even.

The majority of people just weren't used to seeing such pictures as an accurate or naturalistic transcription of what could be perceived (though accuracy of a kind is surely what Monet and Renoir were aiming for). They therefore responded to them as wilful and violent exaggerations.

I've said of the La Grenouillère paintings that the sketchy quality of the brushwork was not particularly remarkable, but the point is it would not have been seen as remarkable in a painting presented *as a sketch,* i.e. a preparatory study for a more finished composition. The more conservative artists and critics saw the Impressionist canvases as unfinished, underworked and thus as professionally incompetent, just as they had earlier dismissed Manet's paintings as if they were *ébauches* presented for judgement as finished works. On the other hand, as we shall see in Part 2, around 1860 progressive writers such as Baudelaire and Théophile Gautier were already warning of the dangers of a 'photographic realism' and finish in painting. The problem, I think, was not that the Impressionists were seen as turning their backs on the aim of naturalistic description (which they were not), but rather that the great majority of their audience were unable to accept that the describing was being competently (or naturalistically) done. ◁

The La Grenouillère paintings were probably not exhibited before 1876, but unfavourable responses to the first Impressionist group exhibition in 1874 (discussed in Part 3 and Radiovision programme 5) expressed the view, familiar now in the history of modern art criticism, that professional traditions were being eroded by casual workmanship. In Leroy's 'Satirical Review' (*Supplementary Documents*, II.1) such judgements were represented in the figure of the fictional Academician, M. Vincent.

> . . . Oh, Corot, Corot, what crimes are committed in your name! It was you who brought into fashion this messy composition, these thin washes, these mud-splashes in front of which the art lover has been rebelling for thirty years and which he has accepted only because constrained and forced by your tranquil stubbornness. Once again, a drop of water has worn away the stone!

And in front of Monet's *Boulevard des Capucines* of 1873 (**Col. pl.II.4**)

> . . . There's impression, or I don't know what it means. Only, be so good as to tell me what those innumerable black tongue-lickings in the lower part of the picture represent?
>   Why, those are people walking along, I replied.
>   . . . But those spots were obtained by the same method as that used to imitate marble: a bit here, a bit there, slap-dash, any old way. It's unheard of, appalling!

A crude version of the development of modernism in art might suggest that there has been a gradual overall shift towards an emphasis on the direct 'creative and expressive response' at the expense of the studied, developed and artificial presentation. There is perhaps some truth in this. But again, some caution is necessary.

In 1865–67, Monet had worked on two large paintings, *Déjeuner sur l'herbe* and *Women in the Garden* (**Pl.II.9**), both clearly intended for exhibition in the Salon. For the first, the dimensions of which were to be approximately 14 x 21 feet, he painted several studies and one complete version of reduced size (**Pl.II.8**, now in the Pushkin Museum, Moscow). As we saw in Block I, these were standard academic procedures for an ambitious composition. The painting was never finished and only fragments remain. The second was painted in broad brushstrokes in a style close to Manet's, but with brighter colour. Monet attempted to work on this painting entirely out of doors, and only when the same lighting conditions prevailed. This presented severe problems of execution, given the time required to paint a picture some $8\frac{1}{2}$ x $6\frac{3}{4}$ feet in size. Such large paintings also represented a considerable financial investment. (Professional models have to be paid, for instance, so Monet was largely dependent on friends and relations to pose for him for both pictures.) *Women in the Garden* was rejected by the 1867 Salon, but was bought by Bazille for 2,500 francs, to be paid in monthly instalments of 50 francs. This was a charitable gesture from a relatively prosperous friend (though Bazille was to die before the entire sum was paid), but the transaction had the result of keeping the painting out of public circulation.

There is strong evidence that Monet and Renoir themselves saw their La Grenouillère paintings, at least initially, as sketches for larger works by which they might hope to attract attention. In September 1869, towards the end of their stay at Croissy, Monet wrote the following to Bazille.

Here I'm at a halt, from lack of paints . . .! Only I this year will have done nothing. This makes me rage against everybody. I'm jealous, mean; I'm going mad. If I could work, everything would go alright. You tell me that it's not fifty, or a hundred francs that will get me out of this [either Bazille was late with his monthly payment, or Monet was trying to get the sum increased]; that's possible, but if you look at it this way, there's nothing for me except to break my head against a wall, because I can't lay claim to any instantaneous fortune . . . I have indeed a dream, a picture of bathing at La Grenouillère, for which I've made some bad sketches, but it's a dream. Renoir, who has been spending two months here, also wants to do this picture.

(Monet to Bazille, 25 September 1869, quoted in Rewald, 1961 pages 227–28.)

▶ What conclusions might be drawn from the information in the two preceding paragraphs and the quotation which follows them? ◀

▷ I suggest the following:

1   That the aim to paint ambitious 'worked-up' pictures for the Salon was one which still preoccupied Monet and Renoir in 1869. (By this time the work done by Courbet and Manet, and the writings of Baudelaire, had become sufficiently well-established among many younger artists for ambitious paintings, even as regards the Salon, to be associated with a 'modern-life' subject and a comparatively informal technique.)

2   That this ambition was practically (and philosophically) in conflict with their aim to work out of doors and to represent subjects in specific lighting conditions. (In 1873 Renoir submitted to the Salon, and had rejected, an $8\frac{1}{2}$ x $7\frac{1}{2}$ feet equestrian portrait, which was entirely conventional in composition and theme. It was certainly not executed out of doors.)

3   That the sheer lack of financial resources (and thus shortage of paint and canvas, and inability to pay models and to rent large studios) made the resolution of this conflict impossible, even had such a resolution been *technically* feasible. ◁

In the event Monet and Renoir made a virtue of the restriction on their working conditions. The La Grenouillère paintings can now be seen as *faits accomplis,* whatever the artists may initially have had in mind. If such sketches could be seen as paintings in their own right, as became apparent after the 1874 Exhibition, from then on the young painters seem to have seen themselves as producing finished paintings with sketch-like qualities. (We should note, however, that once Monet and Renoir came to see their 'sketches' as 'paintings', they were *more* rather than less likely to work over them in the studio.)

It has often happened in the history of modern art that what an artist produced as the contingent result of a complex series of aims and practical circumstances was just what told him or her how to proceed. In Greenberg's terms, 'Impressionist colour, no matter how handled, gave the picture surface its due as a physical entity to a much greater extent than had traditional practice' (Greenberg, 'Cézanne', 1951, page 53), and, 'The logic of the Impressionist readjustment, no matter how reservedly acknowledged, had to work itself out regardless of the volition of individuals' (Greenberg, 'On the Role of Nature in Modernist Painting' 1949, page 171). The idea of a 'logic of readjustment', which has to 'work itself out', suggests a determinist or historicist view of the development of art – a typically Modernist closure on causal systems which must necessarily have been open to alternative possibilities. It is certainly true, however, that from this point on the painters associated with the development of Impressionism would generally accept restriction of size as an inescapable outcome of their technical concerns, and would feel increasingly confident in defending what might have been seen as lack of finish as the necessary means to preserve the integrity of their working procedure and the immediacy of their visual sensations.

Sympathetic critics were soon to follow them in this, particularly those who formed part of the Café Guerbois circle and who were thus participants in the artists' discourse. In 1873, in an introduction to a group exhibition at the Durand-Ruel Gallery, Armand Silvestre wrote,

> What apparently should hasten the success of these newcomers is that their pictures are painted according to a singularly cheerful scale. A 'blond' light floods them and everything in them is gaiety, clarity, spring festival . . .
>
> (Silvestre, introduction to *Galerie Durand-Ruel, recueil d'estampes* (*Collection of Prints*), Paris, 1873, quoted in Rewald, 1961, page 302.)

And a year later, in a considered review of the first Impressionist group exhibition (*Supplementary Documents* II.2), Castagnary gave early expression to what was to become a persistent theme in interpretations of Impressionist art.

> What quick intelligence of the object and what amusing brushwork! True, it is summary, but how just the indications are! . . . The common concept which united them as a group and gives them a collective strength in the midst of our disaggregate epoch is the determination not to search for a smooth execution, to be satisfied with a certain general aspect. Once the impression is captured, they declare their role terminated . . . If one wants to characterize them with a single word that explains their efforts, one would have to create the new term of *Impressionists*. They are impressionists in the sense that they render not a landscape but the sensation produced by a landscape.
>
> (Castagnary, 'Exhibition in the Boulevard des Capucines', *Le Siècle*, 29 April 1874.)

Following such writers as Silvestre and Castagnary and some writings of the artists themselves, Modernist interpretation of Impressionism has tended to emphasize a distinction between the actual landscape and the subjective 'sensation'. The novel technical qualities of Impressionist painting – the broken brushwork and the intensity of colour combined with wide tonal range – are explained as the means to express this sensation, and, as we saw in the Venturi quotation (page 7), this is seen as taking painting in 'a different direction from the Realists'. 'Abstraction from nature' and rejection of the 'significant' subject are seen by Venturi as the qualities in Impressionist painting which give it its place in the origination of 'modern art'. On the question of the Impressionists' interest in reflections, for instance, the American art historian William C. Seitz has this to say:

> Reflections became a means of shaking off the world assembled by memory in favour of a world perceived momentarily by the senses. In reflections the artifices so important to workaday life are transformed into abstract elements in the world of pure vision.
>
> (Quoted by Phoebe Pool, *Impressionism*, pages 86–87)

There is something missing in such accounts, I believe. As was suggested in the *Introduction* the Modernist tends to put emphasis on development in terms of styles, appearances, effects and visions, rather than of problems and of skills deployed to confront them. We will fail to understand adequately either the problems which Monet and Renoir faced in 1869, or the skills they applied in addressing them, if we see their work as belonging in a 'world of pure vision', cut off from the aims of realism or from the problems of representation of a natural and a social world. We need, I believe, to bring subject matter and technique back together, and to consider these as equally significant – as they are likely to have been for the spectator in 1869. At that time at least, the work of Monet and Renoir was still relevant to the persistent problem of how to represent 'modern life'. For the painter, such a problem has to be a *technical* problem if it is to be addressed within his or her practice.

The 'modern life' of the bourgeoisie at leisure had therefore to be given meaning and significance *as modern art,* and by reference to what was significant in other art.

What we *can* say is that in attempting to cope with this problem, and with their own straightened circumstances, Monet and Renoir found themselves producing paintings which did indeed suggest a new direction. The way to proceed, for Monet in particular, may, for certain historians, have seemed to involve concentration not so much upon the scenes of modern social life as upon the more strictly technical problems of representing the phenomenal world as a world variously illuminated, reflected or obscured in the beholder's eye (see **Col. pl.II.5**, Monet, *Autumn at Argenteuil*, 1873). This is how art history has tended to represent the Impressionist project, and Monet has been seen as its typical and principal proponent. According to the Modernist interpretation, Impressionist painting involves a further development in that concentration on (the means of) representing, as against the represented (subject), which Modernist critics find in Manet. There is some justification in this. But it is wrong, I think, to suppose that such an enterprise required the abandonment of all realistic or descriptive concerns. It was to be several years before even Monet's subject matter became largely devoid of identifiable social or class connotations.

▶ Look now at Renoir's *Pont Neuf, Paris* of 1872 (**Col. pl.II.6**). This should help you to test out and to recapitulate some of the points discussed in the preceding section. In particular you should try to decide what problems Renoir has addressed, what interests his choices and decisions suggest, and what skills he has employed. Two particular questions should be borne in mind (we shall return to these issues later):

1   How long do you think such a picture would have taken to paint, given its size?

2   What techniques or resources has Renoir used to decide between or to relate observation, memory and invention in the realization of his picture? ◀

The Impressionist group

I have suggested that the *faits accomplis* of the La Grenouillère paintings gave Monet and Renoir an idea of what to do next. Historical events of more general significance intervened, however, in such a way as to effect a temporary dispersal and regrouping of the younger painters. In July 1870 France declared war on Prussia. A series of defeats led in September to the surrender of Napoleon III at Sedan, and the proclamation of the Third Republic. Paris was under siege by the Prussians from September until the end of January, when the city capitulated. A token occupation by the Prussians was followed in March by the flight of the Republican government to Versailles and the proclamation of a Commune in the capital. Two months later the Versailles government re-entered Paris and repressed the Commune with considerable savagery. Courbet, who had held the post of Curator of Fine Arts under the Commune, was arrested for his part in the destruction of the Vendôme column, and was temporarily imprisoned and heavily fined and exiled. As the politically unstable Third Republic had to pay heavy reparations for the war and undertake the tasks of restoration, a brief boom was followed in 1873 by a bad slump which lasted six years.

Bazille, on whom Monet had depended heavily for support, enlisted in the army under the Republic and was killed in battle in November 1870. Monet himself left for London in 1870 when war broke out and was not to return, via Holland, until the end of 1871. Renoir was drafted into the army in 1870 and became severely ill with dysentery. He was in Paris during the siege and the Commune, as was Berthe Morisot. Degas enlisted in the infantry in 1870, though suffering from impaired vision. During the Commune he stayed with Ingres' patrons, the Valpinçons. Manet joined the Republican National Guard as a staff officer under the painter Meissonier. He was in Paris during the siege (see Figure 1), but in Bordeaux at the time of the Commune. Pissarro left Louveciennes for Brittany in 1870, and travelled from there to England, returning to France in June 1871. Sisley (Pl.II.10) was a British subject and took no part in the war, but it ruined his father, who died in 1871 leaving him without support.

Figure 1 Édouard Manet, The Barricade, *1871, lithograph, 47 cm x 34 cm, 18½ in. x 13½ in. The New York Public Library. Astor, Lenox and Tilden Foundations, Print Division.*

Monet and Pissarro (1831–1903) had met at the Académie Suisse in 1859–60 and had maintained occasional contacts until the later 1860s. In 1869–70 they had often painted together at Bougival and Marly, and after the two painters found themselves together in England, Pissarro was drawn more closely into the Impressionist circle. It was in the years 1871–72 that an Impressionist style emerged as the common factor in the work of several individuals.

One factor in the identification of these artists as a group was the interest shown in their work by the dealer Paul Durand-Ruel, who had moved to London for the duration of the war and the Commune. Durand-Ruel was the main dealer for the Barbizon painters, and when Daubigny introduced him to Monet in London in 1870 he immediately bought paintings from both Monet and Pissarro, whose work he had already seen at the Salon. Like any competent dealer he was no doubt on the look-out for the next development in his own particular line. Back in Paris after the suppression of the Commune, he bought works from Sisley, Renoir and Degas, despite his lack of success with those paintings of Monet's and Renoir's which he had shown in London. From this point on, with the exception of the financially disastrous years from 1874–80, Durand-Ruel consistently supported the Impressionists and bought and exhibited their works when he could.

Between 1872 and 1873 Monet and Renoir were often together again, working side-by-side both in Paris and at Argenteuil, where Monet was then living and where they were joined occasionally by Sisley (see **Col.pl.II.7**: Renoir, *Monet Working in his Garden at Argenteuil*). Pissarro worked nearby at Pontoise (see **Col. pl.II.8**: Pissarro, *Factory near Pontoise*), where Cézanne and Guillaumin joined him in 1872 (**Pls. II.11, II.12**), and at Louveciennes, where he too was visited by Sisley (see map, Figure 2 and Block I Figure 6).

Publicity for their work had become a matter of great importance for the Impressionists by the early 1870s. In accepting the technical implications of their own work of the late 1860s and early 1870s, they were virtually disqualifying themselves from any public success according to the criteria prevailing in the Salon and normally applied to work shown there. Despite the loyalty of Durand-Ruel, this entailed the risk of considerable financial and professional isolation. The sense of community among those with similar problems and interests must therefore have been of critical necessity in the early days of what we now identify as the Impressionist movement. It was also desirable to gain some public recognition of this group identity. If a following could be established, there were benefits to be gained from the need to restrict Impressionist paintings to a small scale: small paintings are easier to sell than large ones.

The formation of an independent exhibiting society, and the organization of their first group exhibition in 1874, can be seen at least in part as long-term consequences of the practical problems which Monet and Renoir faced in 1869 and which they largely shared with others such as Bazille, Sisley and Pissarro.

For several years Monet and his circle had been considering the possibility of an exhibition outside the official Salon which would be privately organized, juryless and would promote the work of all those artists interested in an alternative to the Salon. The Salon was by no means an ideal forum for presenting pictures to the public, quite apart from its prohibitive selection policy (the jury had become more severe and conservative since the suppression of the 1870 Commune) – the lighting was poor, the walls were overcrowded, and pictures insensitively hung. In 1874 this project was finally realized. They were lent suitable premises on two floors on the Boulevard des Capucines, a busy thoroughfare of Haussmann's Paris. The exhibition was presented as work by members of the *Société anonyme des artistes, peintres, sculpteurs, graveurs etc.* (Anonymous society of artists, painters, sculptors, engravers etc.). This was the event now referred to as the 'First Impressionist Exhibition'. Although the *Société* folded up as a formal body after the show had finished, the

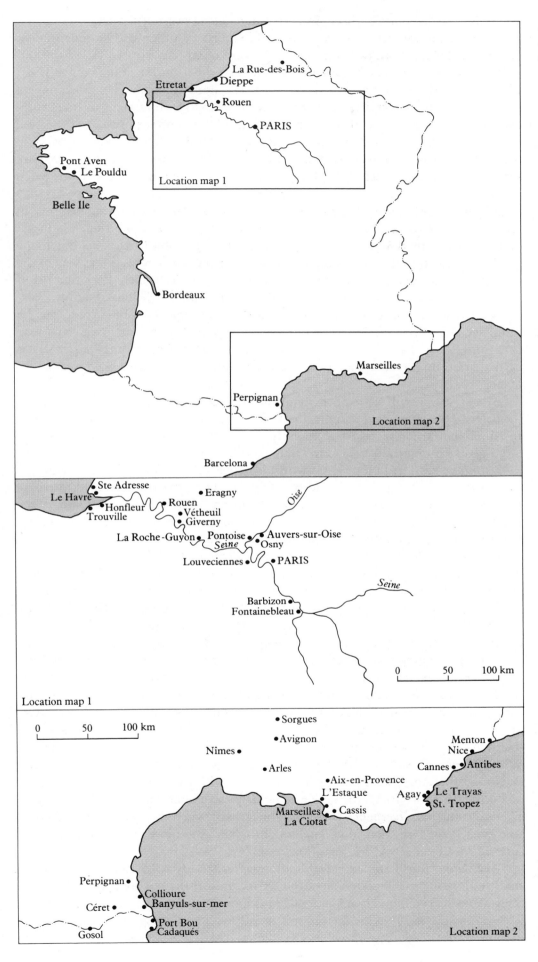

artists involved mounted eight similar exhibitions between 1874 and 1886.

Though the initiative for the public formation of a group and an independent exhibiting organization did come from the core of what was to be called the Impressionist group, it was found necessary and expedient to recruit on a much wider basis. There were various reasons for this: the need to mount an exhibition of sufficient size to attract attention; the need to discharge obligations of friendship, and the need to spread the financial burden. Another important reason was the need to avoid the impression that this was another Salon des Refusés. Participation in such a Salon was no longer acceptable to many. Some of the artists had a body of serious work behind them – in Degas' case, work in the most prestigious Salon genres.

Degas' acquaintance with the group was through Manet whom he had met in 1862, and he took an active part in the organization of the exhibition. He urged caution, insisting that there be a leavening of 'respectable' artists to lessen the emphasis on technical radicalism that Monet wanted to encourage. So, as well as the younger artists, such as Cézanne and Morisot, the exhibition included a number of well-respected artists who had no particular quarrel with the Salon – Boudin, Cals, de Nittis and Latouche for example – which meant that the show could not be dismissed as a substitute Salon des Refusés. However, there were refusals to participate from Corot, Daubigny and Courbet, and, significantly, from the artist whose participation might have been expected and would certainly have been welcomed, Manet.

Manet, as you will remember from Block I, was devoted to the goal of success at the Salon. He saw participation in the *Société anonyme's* exhibition as tantamount to an admission of defeat, and was roundly denounced by Degas as 'more vain than intelligent' for deserting his fellow 'realists'. But it is significant that Manet's motives seem to have had more to do with his beliefs about the mechanism of the art world than his feelings about Monet and friends. He had been accustomed to adopting a senior status among them in his studio on the rue Batignolles and at the nearby Café Guerbois for many years. He certainly took their reputations seriously, urging them to submit work to the Salon with him and to abandon their independent show. To Degas he even wrote 'Exhibit with us; you'll receive an honourable mention'. However, according to M. Elder, there was one artist in the group before whose name he certainly drew the line; 'I'll never commit myself with M. Cézanne'.

The presence in the group of Degas (1834–1917), as well as of the other more conservative artists does serve to moderate the journalistic and more crudely Modernistic accounts of a homogeneous avant-garde, isolated by their commitment to a new and challenging concept of painting. The world of French art in the 1860s and 1870s was not as sharply divided between 'academics' and 'radicals' as such accounts would suggest. We are in danger of misreading the works of Impressionists and comparative conservatives alike if we fail to recognize the wide range of alternative practices possible within that world, and the complexity of the relations between them. As Radiovision programme 4 makes clear, they presented a diverse group. While Monet, Pissarro and Sisley were mainly concerned with landscape, others, Degas most notably, were principally concerned with the figure, while a few, such as Berthe Morisot (Pl.II.13) and Renoir may have appeared to bridge the gap. There was further divergence between those artists, whether of figure or landscape, who treated the city, that most modern of themes, and those who concentrated on rural life – Cézanne and Pissarro, for example.

Although clearly angled towards the market, the first Impressionist show, if anything, weakened the position of the artists *vis à vis* the buying public. Whereas their works had sold quite well at a sale in early 1874, a Pissarro landscape fetching 940 francs, by 1875, once the group's name and notoriety as 'intransigents' had become established, buyers were reluctant to risk their money. Simultaneously

Durand-Ruel cut back on his purchases, partly due to the financial recession. This was an outcome that Theodore Duret, critic and early supporter of the Impressionists, had predicted when he warned his friend Pissarro to stay out of the fray such an exhibition would undoubtedly cause. Despite the consequent financial insecurity however, Pissarro seems to have relished the notoriety and unpopularity associated with being an 'intransigent', whereas Renoir resented being dubbed a revolutionary and did not feel himself to be one. Degas for his part disliked being classed with the landscape painters as an 'Impressionist' and preferred the more neutral title, 'Independent'.

Those who showed in the first group exhibition were joined far more by a need to attract a public, and to secure better showing conditions than prevailed in the Salon, than they were by some consistent radicalism in their art. Among a minority of this group, difficulty in selling and exhibiting work was in part attributable to novelty of style, but the comparative poverty of Monet and Renoir reflected rather the difficulty anyone was likely to face in being petit-bourgeois and trying to be an artist, than that of being an artist who painted in a new style.

Claude Monet

The Modernist view of Impressionism as an avant-garde movement within a history of autonomous technical concerns depends very strongly both on establishing Monet as the central figure in the Impressionist project, and on the promotion of a particular interpretation of Monet's work. It is possible that Monet is established as the 'major Impressionist' within Modernist art history precisely because he presents the best case for a Modernist view of Impressionism.

In the 1880s when the Impressionists ceased to be a coherent group, Monet began increasingly to concentrate on the effects of changing light, and he did certainly *pick out* subjects which first and foremost offered opportunity for analysis and representation of those effects. These tended to be subjects which could be represented under different conditions – poplar trees, haystacks, the facade of Rouen Cathedral and finally his own water garden at Giverny (**Col. pl.II.9**) – rather than scenes to which any significance might be attached as moments in social life. But however vividly the appearances of these later paintings seem to advertise Monet's compulsive engagement with their own surfaces, they can still be read as complex assemblages of signs, which signify some plausible and discriminating experience of the actual world.

The study of reflections on a ruffled surface of water, for instance, may tend to encourage a broken and all-over paint surface. (Though as Anthea Callen shows in Television programme 4, there is more variety in Monet's brushwork than such a view of his work might suggest. This variety, moreover, is clearly linked to differences in what he was actually looking at and seeking to represent.) If we follow Monet's work from the La Grenouillère painting (**Col. pl.II.1**) through *Impression, Sunrise* (**Col. pl.II.10**) and *Autumn at Argenteuil* (**Col. pl.II.5**) to the last paintings of lily ponds (**Col. pl.II.9**), we might say that representations of such ruffled surfaces tend to occupy an increasingly large proportion of the picture surface, until they come to fill it altogether in certain of the late paintings. On the basis of these paintings, Modernist criticism has seen Monet as an important figure in the development of the autonomous 'all-over', expressive picture. (William Rubin, in an influential series of articles on the development of Jackson Pollock, accorded Monet a significant influence over the American painter's 'all-over' abstract paintings of 1947–50.) But, in this, Modernists have neglected that perspective offered by Castagnary, by which Monet could be seen as working within the framework of the contemporary debate on 'realism'/'naturalism'. See, in this connection, Duret's assessment of Monet (*Supplementary Documents*, II.5).

We could alternatively explain this development in Monet's work as the result of an increasing concentration on certain technical problems of descriptive representation. A surface of water seen under natural conditions is not something that can normally be set up in the studio. Cabanel's *Birth of Venus* (**Col. pl.I.8**) and Manet's *Battle of 'Kearsarge' and 'Alabama'* (**Pl. I.71**) from Block I offer examples of representations of water contrived in the studio. These painters had to employ inventive techniques in a manner somehow consistent with the overall character of their brushwork and of the picture surface, in order to persuade the spectator that water was what was being represented. Monet also had to do this (as was pointed out in the *Introduction, all* representation involves invention and codification), but by practising painting direct from nature in the open air, he was able to develop techniques of a different kind, adapted to the actual scenes before him and requiring the rapid application of comparatively unblended and unmodulated colours. (He and Renoir were greatly assisted in this by the comparatively recent availability of oil colours in airtight tubes, ready-mixed to a certain consistency.) Monet practised these techniques over several decades and undoubtedly became very good at them.

It is all very well to talk about painting one's sensations before nature. But let us say that having painted one picture of the scene before him, the artist then paints a second (as Monet often did). The second picture is likely to be as much a 'response' to the first picture – and to what was *learned* in doing it – as it is to the original scene. It will be at least as much concerned with *painting*, and with *knowledge* about painting, as it is with natural phenomena, subjective sensations, impressions of light and atmosphere, or the expression of feeling. For an artist, a technique is a way of memorizing what one sees, and of learning how to represent what one has remembered. If you try yourself to draw an outdoor scene, you will soon discover how much of the varied information it offers can be forgotten even in the instant it takes for your focus to change from landscape to sheet of paper. (In the light of the discussion in this paragraph, look back at Renoir's *Pont Neuf, Paris* (**Col. pl.II.6**), and check your answers to the questions I asked about it on page 16.)

By the time he came to paint his last pictures of lily ponds, Monet was able to do what he had struggled unsuccessfully to do in the mid-1860s: paint large, modern pictures of outdoor scenes, though of course by then the meaning of 'the modern' had changed, and he himself had helped to change it. And where he had earlier been restricted by lack of financial resources, he was now wealthy and powerful enough to direct a stream through his own property and to make an ideal studio of his entire garden. (This garden, and the paintings Monet made there, will be shown and discussed in Televison programme 4.)

We may here observe a characteristic tactic of Modernist art history. Monet's financial condition in 1869 is not seen as having *disenabled* him from painting the more conventional pictures he seems to have wished to paint. He is merely seen as having 'transcended' those conditions 'for the sake of his art'. Nor are the more conventionally ambitious – if not technically conventional – paintings of his last years seen as *enabled* in any significant way by his improved financial conditions, although he could certainly not have painted these pictures had he not been wealthy. In both cases his 'art' is separated out from his 'life' in such a way that the economic circumstances of the latter have no real explanatory role to play in establishing the expressive significance of the former.

The overall point I wish to make is this. The problems of representing light and reflections on ruffled water were sufficiently interesting to engage Monet at intervals over some fifty years. It is unlikely that this would have been the case had these apparently specialized interests not allowed Monet also to engage with concerns central to his interest in modern painting and his wish to be a part of its development. But we should not confuse talking about Monet with talking about the Impressionist project as a whole, nor should we talk about his art as if it were somehow self-propelling and indifferent to circumstances and alternatives. Other Impressionists pursued other interests, in part prompted no doubt by other ideas about what the central concerns of modern painting were or should be. Camille Pissarro, for instance, was a central figure in the Impressionist group. He is not noted for his paintings of reflections on ruffled water. And it has only been in comparatively recent years that his work has received an attention matching that devoted to Monet. Yet I think a case can be made for placing his activity as close to the 'central concerns of modern painting' as Monet's. This depends, of course, on how one identifies these central concerns. We will return to Pissarro.

As we have seen, Modernist criticism has tended to represent the pursuit of 'realism' as incompatible with an emphasis upon subjective 'sensations', and the Impressionists, therefore, as turning the tide of realistic description in pursuit of autonomy for the expressive pictorial surface. This seems like a retrospective rationalization, and one which makes of the Impressionists a more homogeneous group than they were. We should remember, for instance, that Cézanne showed in the First Impressionist group exhibition (though in only one of the later exhibitions). Lampooning his rejected submissions to the 1870 Salon, a journalist wrote,

> Cézanne hails from Aix-en-Provence. He is a realist painter and, what is more, a convinced one. Listen to him rather, telling me with a pronounced Provençal accent: 'Yes, my dear Sir, I paint as I see, as I feel – and I have very strong sensations. The others, too, feel and see as I do, but they don't dare . . . They produce Salon pictures . . . I dare, Sir, I dare . . . I have the courage of my opinions – and he laughs best who laughs last.'
> (Quoted in J. Rewald, 'Un article inédit sur Paul Cézanne en 1870', *Arts,* Paris, July 21–27, 1954)

What this quotation demonstrates is that in 1870, at least, 'realism' (i.e. working 'according to nature') and the primacy of subjective 'sensation' were not necessarily seen as inconsistent. However, as we saw, Castagnary predicted this separation in 1874, but it was not to become generally evident until the 1880s, when it was made in the literary and artistic theory of Symbolism, as we shall see in the next block. From then on, Monet's work in particular tended to be interpreted retrospectively as showing the results of a concern with 'sensation' over description, and as demonstrating the expressive autonomy of the painted surface. He became the 'important Impressionist' at least in part because his work seemed relevant to the next avant-garde phase. But by the 1880s the Impressionist project had broken down into a series of individual and diverse practices. (You should now read the section in Hamilton on Renoir's later work, pages 27–34, which should help to demonstrate why Monet's name remained more firmly linked with Impressionism than his.)

Camille Pissarro

Though, as we have observed, Monet is normally singled out as the 'paradigm Impressionist' within Modernist accounts of the movement, we have chosen to concentrate rather on Pissarro in the broadcasts associated with this block (Television programme 5 and Radiovision programme 6). We have done so in order to examine some of the problems which such accounts raise or ignore, and in order to reintroduce some of the historical issues relevant to a wider understanding of the Impressionist project and of its 'crisis' (or crises) in the 1880s (discussed more fully in the next block). This section is intended to provide some background to the broadcasts, and to establish some links between the work of Pissarro and the Impressionist movement as a whole.

When Pissarro returned to France in June 1871 it was to discover that of some 1500 works which he had left at Louveciennes, only about 40 remained following the Prussian occupation, when his house had been used as a butcher's shop. The loss of so substantial a proportion of his work of the later 1860s inhibits comparison with Monet's and Renoir's of the same period, and may have encouraged an emphasis on their role as the initiators of Impressionism.

▶ Pissarro's *Coach at Louveciennes* (**Col. pl.II.11**), dated 1870 and painted before his departure for Brittany, is a work typical of the early phase of Impressionism. Compare it to the La Grenouillère paintings by Renoir and Monet and note the common features. ◀

▷ It should be clear that Pissarro has adopted a similarly wide tonal range. The painting aims to represent a specific and momentary effect of light and weather, and the light, broken brushwork suggests a similarly rapid execution. He has also shown interest in the reflections of light from water, though in this case it is the surface of a roadway under heavy rain. There is more of Corot's sobriety in this painting than you could find in either Monet or Renoir, I think (**Pl.II.14**), and there is clearly no sense of the holiday atmosphere which pervades their work at this time. Pissarro has painted what might be the scene outside his own front door, whereas Monet and Renoir had travelled to Croissy in order to paint scenes of a particular character associated with such places. One last point of possible difference: the woman on the right has her umbrella up, suggesting that the rain is still falling. We might ask whether Pissarro would really have painted his picture out of doors in the rain. This leads us to consider the role of technical procedures in structuring the relation between noticing and painting. I suggest that the execution of this picture took place in the studio, and that unlike those done at La Grenouillère it would probably have required some form of preliminary drawing or sketch. ◁

Pissarro was born into a bourgeois Jewish family in the Virgin Islands in 1830, two years before Manet, and he came to Paris in 1855. He spent some time at the École des Beaux-Arts, and worked in the 1860s as an exponent of the current modern version of the French rural landscape tradition associated with Millet, Corot and the Barbizon (see Radiovision programme 8). He exhibited eleven paintings in the Salon between 1859 (when Manet and Whistler were among those rejected and when Monet arrived in Paris) and 1870, as well as showing in the Salon des Refusés, and he attracted the praise of Zola and Castagnary. In his successful submissions of 1864 and 1865 he labelled himself a 'pupil of Corot'. *L'Hermitage at Pontoise* of 1867 (**Pl.II.15**) is a good example of his work in the later part of the decade. L'Hermitage was the part of Pontoise in which he lived between 1866 and 1868.

▶ Compare this painting with *Bourgeois House at l'Hermitage, Pontoise* (**Col. pl.II.12**) of 1873. Note what seem to you the significant differences and similarities. ◀

▷ What I particularly note is that where the earlier painting is separated into three principal planes – the foreground, the row of houses in the centre, with their different flat surfaces strongly marked by contrasts of tone, and the hill rising towards the skyline in the distance – the spatial relations in the later painting are more complicated and broken. In the latter the distinctness of individual forms is 'dissolved' by the character of the brushwork, which is both more consistent and more consistently agitated. It is a more typically 'Impressionistic' picture. So far the Modernist interpretation of Impressionism receives some support. Yet there is one feature common to both paintings which also deserves mention: the relation of the figures to their surroundings. A rampantly Modernist view would encourage us to see the figures in the second painting essentially as brushstrokes within a world of brushstrokes, integrated more successfully than the stooping peasants of the first into the overall decorative scheme of the picture surface. To accept such a view, I think, is to rob Pissarro's paintings of their specificity, and to impose on oneself a form of 'aspect-blindness' (see *Introduction*, page 37). The evidence of Pissarro's drawings is that the figures of his paintings were based on careful studies of individuals and types, and that many of these show peasants at work in the fields and on their smallholdings. A comparison of the left-hand figure in a drawing of 1874–76 **(Pl.II.16)** with the right-hand figure in the 1867 painting is an example of Pissarro's tendency to single out specific physical attitudes clearly signifying rural labour. ◁

It was not until the 1880s that Pissarro was to make such figures the major subjects of his paintings. (This later phase of his activity is discussed by T.J. Clark in Television programme 5.) Yet in the great majority of his landscapes before this time the presence of figures is significant, however small a space they may occupy within the overall composition. They are far more than mere decorative or anecdotal additions, I believe. I would even go so far as to say that where figures are absent from Pissarro's paintings, their very absence is usually significant. Look at *Factory near Pontoise* **(Col. pl.II.8)** for instance. Pissarro painted four pictures on this theme, showing a large factory constructed in the early 1860s and extended in 1872–73. (It had been built for the distilling of alcohols from sugar beet grown locally by peasants such as those shown in his other paintings.) In each of them the factory is shown from across the river, with no bank visible in the foreground. There is, as it were, no distinct space for the familiar peasants to inhabit. (In this case the distant cart and figure *can* more plausibly be seen to have their principal identity as mere brushstrokes.) In Television programme 6, Griselda Pollock and Fred Orton discuss the dislocating effects of industrialization on peasant communities in connection with Van Gogh's painting of the *Potato Eaters*. (An alternative, and more 'Modernistic', explanation might be that in making a subject of the factory, Pissarro was merely responding to the need to evoke modern themes; and that he 'returned' to pictures in which the peasant could be relocated as a central and dominant subject for the 'technical' reason that the factory paintings, with their central composition and frontal emphasis, looked inadequately sophisticated in relation to the compositions of his contemporaries.)

In Television programme 5, Tim Clark draws attention to Pissarro's tendency to locate his peasant figures in relation to information about the conditions of their life and labour. In *L'Hermitage at Pontoise,* for instance, the relation between the figures and their environment is established not simply by the nature of their activity as it is represented, but also by the strip-cultivation which patterns the distant hillside. In the *Bourgeois House,* though the picture space may be more closely integrated as such, the long wall serves clearly to separate two social worlds, two classes and forms of life, one represented as closeted and impenetrable, the other as overlooked and public.

I do not mean to suggest that Pissarro's art was intentionally 'political' at this point, though Tim Clark and Christopher Lloyd in Television programme 5 and Radiovision programme 6 respectively do demonstrate that Pissarro's attitude to his art and his ambitions for it were clearly affected by his political views in the 1880s and 1890s. What does seem clear is that Pissarro's paintings – even his most typically Impressionist paintings – are structured by his means of perceiving the world he inhabited, and that the nature of that perception cannot simply be characterized in terms of his 'responses to nature' on the one hand and his 'autonomous technical concerns' on the other. From very early in his career – at least from the mid-1860s – Pissarro's perception of the world was a critical perception of a *social* world, one in which different classes of people led different lives, engaged in different activities, and had different types of relation to their surroundings. His perception of the landscape was as a series of *places* which had been shaped by those lives, activities and relations, and which had also, in the case of the peasants, determined what those lives and activities were like. The relation of landscape and figure seems specific and interesting in Pissarro's Impressionist paintings. The one serves to contextualise and to inform about the other. This is done by painting and *as* (modern) painting. As I say, I do not intend to define Pissarro as a 'political artist'. My point is rather that how anyone perceives the world, and how they subsequently represent it, will have political determinations and implications.

Pissarro's view of the social world he inhabited can defensibly be read out of his paintings, I believe. What we should not do is make assumptions about the politics of artists and then read these back *into* their paintings in pursuit of consistent expressive meanings. Pissarro has the reputation of an anarchist, Degas of a conservative. On this basis we might expect their art to represent incompatible views of the nature and construction of the social world. Yet Pissarro and Degas had in common an interest in the lives of working people, at least as subjects for their art. The two artists began to collaborate on printmaking in 1879, at the outset of a period of political polarization in France. Degas introduced Pissarro to a wide range of experimental techniques, was clearly generous with his own facilities and resources, and himself printed many of Pissarro's plates over the next three years. Richard Brettell has claimed that 'The artist who stood behind Pissarro in the 1880s was Edgar Degas . . . who provided the impetus for this entire phase of Pissarro's career'. ('Camille Pissarro: a Revision', in *Camille Pissarro 1830–1903*, exhibition catalogue, Arts Council of Great Britain and the Museum of Fine Arts, Boston, 1980.) It was these two, older than the others, who were largely responsible for the organizational work of the Impressionist group, who provided the impetus for its eight exhibitions over twelve years, and who maintained the possibility of change and development within that group by making sure that younger artists were brought in. Cézanne and Guillaumin were included in the first exhibition at Pissarro's insistence (and the former in the face of considerable opposition; it was not only within the Salon that he was seen as an embarrassing incompetent). Pissarro introduced Gauguin in 1879 and Seurat and Signac in 1886. The American artist Mary Cassatt was invited to join by Degas in 1877, as were other figure painters in subsequent exhibitions. Renoir and Sisley showed in only four of the group exhibitions, Monet in only five. Degas missed only one (in 1882), though he was less dependent than any of the other principals on income from sales. Pissarro was the only artist to show work in all eight exhibitions.

In Tahiti in 1895, Gauguin wrote in his notebook,

> If we observe the totality of Pissarro's work, we find there, despite fluctuations, not only an extreme artistic will, never belied, but also an essentially intuitive, pure-bred art . . . He looked at everybody, you say! Why not? Everyone looked at him, too, but denied him. He was one of my masters and I do not deny him.
>
> (Quoted in Rewald, 1961, page 575)

And in his submission to two group exhibitions at Aix in 1902 and 1906, by which time he was established in France as a major modern painter, Cézanne recognized the debt he owed to Pissarro's persistent friendship and support by designating himself 'pupil of Pissarro'.

2 Edgar Degas

Degas and Modernism

Degas has been chosen as the subject for the case study in this block because he allows us to examine the tendency of Modernistic accounts of Impressionism to divorce the progressive and increasingly 'autonomous' technical concerns from 'realistic' and 'modern-life' concerns. More specifically, this block will consider:

1   The association between Degas and Manet and the continuity of concern for 'modern-life' subjects from Manet to Degas, emphasizing the realistic strain in French art. Such a perspective may help to counter the prevailing Modernist account which singles out Monet, but accords Degas an essentially marginal, though worthy, position;

2   Degas' intense and professional concern with problems of descriptive representation, which encourages us to moderate the view of later nineteenth-century French art as an important stage in the development of art towards abstraction and technical autonomy;

3   His use of photography, which raises issues of direct relevance to contemporary debates about realism and the function and future of descriptive and 'documentary' skills in art.

The following quotation provides an example of the normal Modernist view of Degas' position in relation to the other Impressionist painters with whom he showed in the first group exhibition in 1874.

> Degas had little in common with the 'Impressionists' in the group. He was primarily interested in painting the human figure; Monet, Pissarro, Sisley and to some extent Renoir, were mainly occupied with landscape. He was at heart a draughtsman and they were painters, colourists. He believed that a work of art stemmed from the painter's imagination and should be done from memory in the studio; they believed that a work of art should accurately reflect what the painter sees and should be done directly in front of the subject or motif. He believed in perception; they believed in observation. The sketchiness of his pictures stemmed from his training as a draughtsman, a discipline which encourages the rapid sketch and allows the artist to be spontaneous in the way he first puts down his ideas on paper. The landscape artists in the exhibition appeared 'sketchy' . . . because of the system of painting in dabs of pigment, short comma-like brushstrokes, in an attempt to capture the fleeting colours they saw in 'light'; their sketchiness stemmed from being painters, not draughtsmen.
>
> (Ian Dunlop, *Degas,* 1979, page 125.)

This is a simplified account (we might, for instance, wish to question Dunlop's implied contrast between imagination and perception on the one hand, and observation on the other), but a casual comparison of Degas' *The Absinthe Drinker* (Col. pl.II.13) and Monet's *Boulevard des Capucines* (Col. pl.II.4) will reveal immediately several of the differences which Dunlop describes. They are, of course, very different subjects, but the differences are largely typical. Whereas Monet shows an outdoor scene of Parisian life, Degas shows an interior scene which concentrates on the figures inhabiting it. We know that Degas used two friends as models, which tells us something about how the scene was contrived (though it may well have been contrived to represent an actual and remembered scene or circumstance). The colour in the Degas seems more subdued and the different colours seem to have been blended. The Monet appears brighter, with greater contrasts of tone. The handling of the paint seems different. It is characteristic of Degas' painting technique at this date to employ broad expanses of comparatively flat colour rather than to stipple the surface with small brushstrokes in differing colours as in the Monet painting. Where you are aware of Degas' brushwork it looks as though he is using the brush to draw with, for instance in the outline of the right shoulder of the seated woman. Of course, what may be meant by drawing is not easily restricted to particular technical means (see, for instance, the extract in the *Supplementary Documents*, II.7). Drawing appears to be a minor concern for Monet.

A brief glance at the captions of the *Café Concert* and the two paintings of *The Rehearsal of the Ballet on Stage* (Col. pls.II.14,15,16), which describe the media variously used as oil mixed with turpentine, pastel over brush and ink, and pastel over monotype, will indicate another important distinguishing characteristic of Degas' artistic practice, namely the varied range of his techniques. He seems to have been more willing to explore a wide range of genres and techniques than many of the Impressionists.

Unless he is to be seen merely as a conservative, Degas seems to present difficulties for an account of modern art which treats Impressionism as the dominating avant-garde movement of the time. Certain aspects of Degas' artistic practice have nevertheless been singled out as progressive and as anticipating later developments in modern art.

▶ Please read the following extracts in order to gain an idea of what these might be.

> Manet and Degas insisted on fitting what they saw of the brilliant passing show into a language of pattern, of attentuated shapes of infinitely subtle colour relationships disengaged from a particular moment in time. At heart they were both — to use a modern term — abstract artists.
> (Samuel Lane Faison, *Edouard Manet,* 1953, quoted in Phoebe Pool, *Impressionism.*)

> Not only is the nude here purely a pretext for the representation of space and form, but the relationship of the colours is boldly arranged in a series of variations of whites and blues.
> (Sandra Orienti, *Degas,* 1969, page 37.)

> His pastels became multicoloured fireworks where all precision of form disappeared in favour of a texture that glittered with hatchings.
> (John Rewald, *History of Impressionism,* 1980, page 666.) ◀

▷ All three statements suggest that in Degas' work, interest in the decorative possibilities of line, pattern, colour and texture take precedence over the descriptive, mimetic possibilities of his subject matter. Rewald's comment on Degas' late pastels suggests that his work was a pretext for an exercise in the elaboration of the painted surface. As was suggested in the *Introduction,* the view of the subject as mere 'pretext' for exercises in colour and form is typical of Modernist interpretations of late-nineteenth century French art. If you study the *Café Concert* (Col. pl.II.14), despite the fact that you are being asked to look at the glossy surface of an illustration, there is enough observable detail in the different coloured strokes for you to get a sense of the richly worked texture that Degas was clearly interested in exploring in this work. Similarly, if you look at the oil painting,(**Col. pl.II.**17), and subordinate your recognition of the horses and riders that Degas has represented, you may find that it is possible to describe the scene in terms of 'pure design', particularly if you concentrate on the colour relationships of the jockeys' silks to their surroundings. This effect of flat, coloured pattern is underlined by Degas' use of the oil medium, where he has thinned his pigment with spirit and applied it in thin transparent layers which allow a recognition of the material presence of the support. However, this exercise shows how such an approach limits our understanding of why the painting is as it is, as well as the dangers of 'reading in' described in the *Introduction*. ◁

We should not assume that those technical effects and interests which such an analysis singles out were necessarily seen by Degas as independent from an interest in particular types of subject. Nevertheless what has been established is that Degas' work is distinctive in a number of interesting ways which both identify him and set him apart from his Impressionist colleagues. We need to consider this individuality in the light of historical evidence of Degas' social background, professional relations with the Impressionist group, training and technical experiment. This is the principal aim of this case study. In order to give further coherence the case study will concentrate principally on Degas' activity between 1870–88; the period when he established the main characteristics of his compositions and was involved socially and professionally with the Impressionists.

Degas' social and artistic background

Social milieu

The nature of his upbringing and social class may help to explain Degas' particular relationship with the Impressionist group. He was born in 1834, four years after Pissarro and two years after Manet, the eldest son of a banker whose family had Italian as well as French antecedents. His mother was the daughter of a successful businessman from New Orleans. (**Pl.II.**17 shows a group portrait of Degas' relatives and their business associates in their place of business in New Orleans.) Degas was born into the *haute bourgeoisie* (upper middle class) at a time when the successful members of that class had amassed considerable commercial fortunes. To be the son of a banker was to have certain social and cultural advantages. Degas went to the Lycée Louis le Grand, one of the three Lycées in Paris which prepared young men for the École Normale Supérieure, France's elite educational institution. He there made friends with Henri Rouart, who later became an eminent engineer, metallurgist and connoisseur of art, and with whom Degas was to have fruitful professional connections (he also exhibited at a number of Impressionist exhibitions).

His father Auguste De Gas, a cultivated man and lover of music and art, took his son to the Louvre at an early age. Before Degas was twenty, his father had introduced him to some of the most eminent collectors in Paris, Louis La Caze, Eudoxe Marcille, Prince Nicholas Soutzo (who taught him etching), and Henri Valpinçon, an enthusiastic patron of Ingres and owner of his *Odalisque with the Turban*, known as *Valpinçon's Bather* (*Baigneuse de Valpinçon*, **Pl.II.**18). It was through Valpinçon that Degas met Ingres in about 1855. This wealthy and cultured background tended to set Degas apart from the other members and associates of the Impressionist group, with the exception of Manet and Berthe Morisot who

Figure 3   Edgar Degas, Degas salutant *(Self Portrait),
1862, oil on canvas, 92 cm x 69 cm, 36¼ in x 27 in.
Courtesy Calouste Gulbenkian Foundation Museum,
Lisbon.*

were also from the *haute bourgeoisie.* In the portrait of Degas' father listening to
Pagans playing the guitar (**Pl.II.19**), evidence of the wealth and culture of his
family background is clearly detectable. Neither Renoir's nor Monet's father is
likely to have been in a position to invite this popular singer and guitarist into their
own homes.

Degas' training

In order to consider whether Degas' artistic practice was significantly different from
the Impressionists, we require information on where and how Degas received his
training in artistic skills. It will then be possible to consider more fully the question
of his distinctive style.

Degas was originally destined by his father for a career in the respectable profes-
sion of the law (as Matisse was to be later). However Degas' father recognized his
son's talent in art and in 1854 conceded to his ambitions and allowed him to attend
the studio of Louis Lamothe. In the previous year Degas' name appears as one of the
students allowed to copy from the engravings by Dürer, Mantegna, Goya and Rem-
brandt held at the Cabinet des Estampes in the Louvre. Among the products of such
study was a copy of Marcantonio Raimondi's engraving of Raphael's lost *Judgement
of Paris* (**Pl.II.20** see also **Pl.I.61**). By coincidence the same figures were copied by
Manet and used as a model for his *Déjeuner sur l'Herbe* (cf. **Col.pl.I.1**). Louis
Lamothe was a disciple of Ingres who in his programme of tuition transmitted to
Degas the technical precepts of this authoritative figure. Unlike Manet, who spent
five years in the studio of Thomas Couture, Degas was in Lamothe's studio for just a
year and then enrolled in the École des Beaux Arts, which you will recall was the
principal academic art school in Paris. Degas later expressed dislike of the École,
but nevertheless he appears to have been prepared to follow the teaching programme of drawing and copying: first making copies from engravings of classical sculpture, then drawings of plaster casts and finally of the life model. Degas' notebooks

for the period 1859–64 show many copies after the Old Masters and from classical sculptures (**Pls II.21,22**). Degas was fortunate in having independent means and was therefore spared the effort of having to compete for the Prix de Rome (established, like the Rome Prize in England, to allow promising students from the principal academies to study 'classical art' at first hand). Instead he was able to spend long periods in Italy staying with his Italian relatives in Naples and Florence and frequenting the circle of the Villa Medici, seat of the French Academy in Rome.

In Italy he executed many copies using the most diverse works as models: Signorelli's frescoes in Orvieto, Giotto at Assisi, Fra Angelico in Florence. In *Shop Talk,* Degas is later reported as expressing his enormous respect for the work of the Old Masters and the benefit that he derived from studying them. 'No art was ever less spontaneous than mine. What I do is the result of the reflection and the study of the great masters.' 'Try for the spirit and love of Mantegna combined with the dash and colouring of Veronese.' (Quoted by Elizabeth Holt in the *Documentary History of Art,* 1966, Vol.III, pages 401, 403.) **Pl.II.23** provides an example of an attempt by Degas to secure the lively brushwork and rich colour of the sixteenth-century Venetian painter, Veronese, by studying a detail of the Venetian painter's *Finding of Moses* which was then housed in the Musée des Beaux Arts, Lyons. (Manet also painted a study of the same picture.) On his return to Paris to take up permanent residence as a practising artist, Degas concentrated his efforts on producing portraits and on the respected genre of the large-scale history painting.

▶ Please examine Degas' *Young Spartan Girls Provoking the Boys* (**Col. pl.II.18**), which provides an example of one such work, taking note of the preparatory study for the young boy (**Pl.II.24**). What features appear conventional to you in terms of academic painting? What features appear novel? ◀

▷ Degas follows academic convention in his choice of a classical subject, an incident from Greek history when Lycurgus ordered Spartan girls to engage in wrestling contests with youths.

Degas clearly made many drawings and studies in preparation for the final canvas. In this preparatory process he probably used copies from other works of art. In one of his notebooks he referred to a drawing by the sixteenth-century Italian artist, Pontormo, in relation to this picture. Though the painting was left unfinished, it is clear that the composition of the figures was carefully considered. The two main groups and the subsidiary third group in the background have been skilfully balanced and contrasted. Poses of individual figures are likewise repeated and diversified. Despite these considerations, the animation and comparatively 'modern' appearance of the figures, and the sketchy application of the paint, would have distinguished the painting from the more conventionally classical subjects common in the Salon at this time. Degas seems not to have submitted the picture to the Salon, perhaps because it was unfinished, and when he exhibited it in the Fifth Impressionist Exhibition in 1880 he was careful to date it as an early work. ◁

As the examination of Degas' early history painting has revealed, Degas was an artist who characteristically employed a systematic programme of preparation for any artistic project in which he was involved. This type of preparatory work had been established during the Renaissance in order for artists to deal competently with large-scale collaborative projects. As you learnt in Block I, by the nineteenth century this programme had been codified and enforced in a comparatively unimaginative way. In the following discussion of Degas' working methods two generalizations should be kept in mind. Throughout his working life, Degas appears to have adhered to the habits of observing and recording – a practice first established by his academic training. And, more significantly, he was prepared to work out new procedures based on a variety of techniques in order to meet the demands of personal projects that interested him. In contrast to such typically Modernist views as Rewald's, we might argue not that his subjects were pretexts for technical exercises, but rather that his technical innovations were closely related to his interest in modernizing the subject matter of art. We shall explore this relationship in more detail later, in particular in considering his use of photography.

Manet and Degas

Although Degas is normally associated with work he produced after 1870, he was active during the 1860s, the decade in which Manet established his reputation. In fact Degas was only two years younger than Manet.

From the same generation and from similar social origins both artists can be seen to have shared a respect for traditional practices like history painting and mastery of technical processes – those of the Old Masters and those regarded as innovative by contemporaries (for Manet, Spanish painting, Couture and the *ébauche* (see Block I); for Degas, Italian Renaissance painting, the revised status of the sketch and techniques like monotype, oil wash and mixed media). They also took their themes and subjects from compatible sources, which can be closely related to Baudelaire's notion of *modernité* and its heroism;

> . . . the majority of artists who have concerned themselves with really modern subjects have contented themselves with the certified, official subjects, with our victories and our political heroism . . . yet there are subjects from private life which are heroic in quite another way.
>
> The spectacle of elegant life and of the thousands of irregular existences led in the basements of a big city by criminals and kept women . . . we need only open our eyes to recognize our heroism.
>
> (*Salon of 1846,* see Block I, page 21)

It is the realism of Manet and Degas that Modernists have most difficulty in explaining; they do so by claiming that these artists' subjects and themes do not constitute the most important aspect of their art,

> . . . Manet's art has always been open to contradictory interpretations: the contradictions reside in the conflict between his ambitions and his actual situation (what one takes to be the salient features of his situation is open to argument; an uncharacteristically subtle Marxist could, I think, make a good case for focusing on the economic and political situation in France after 1848 . . .) Manet's art represents the last attempt in Western painting to achieve a full equivalent to the great realistic painting of the past: an attempt which led, in quick inexorable steps, to the founding of Modernism through the emphasis on pictorial qualities and problems in their own right.
>
> (M. Fried *Three American Painters,* Reader, page 121)

Modernists are aware of the choices but regard formal qualities as the motive force for change in modern painting. As we have seen in Block I, for any historically adequate explanation of Manet's paintings, his works have to be seen in terms of the forces and contradictions in Napoleon III's France. Fried's stress on 'pictorial qualities and problems in their own right' can be faulted on these grounds, but, as the Degas case study will attempt to show, it can also be faulted in its claim that Manet's paintings 'represent the last attempt in Western painting to achieve a full equivalent to the great realistic painting of the past'. The continuing preoccupation with a form of realism, as instanced by Manet, Degas, Pissarro, Seurat and the

Cubists is one that Modernists disregard. And from the Degas material in this Block and Radiovision programme 4, *Images of Prostitution* you should be able to note the close links between Manet's and Degas' themes – from the representation of contemporary and class-specific women to the general themes of Baudelairean *modernité*. We are not claiming that Manet and Degas constituted a well organized group concerned with the pursuit of themes associated with realism, but that their paintings and their conversations with other artists, as in the Café Guerbois, contributed to a tradition in French painting that can be seen as a strong and central preoccupation.

(One fact that illustrates the artistic, if not personal, link between Manet and Degas is the fate of the dismembered version of the *Execution of Maximilian,* now in the National Gallery, London. In Block I you gained a picture of its social, political and artistic references; a history painting on a contemporary theme, evoking aspects aimed at a criticism of Napoleon III's government. After the painting was cut up, pieces of it were acquired from Manet's family by Vollard and Portier. The family had decided to sell pieces of it as separate examples of 'genre' figures (!). Degas bought these pieces from the dealers and, after considerable effort, acquired by 1902 all that remained of the painting and mounted the fragments on a new canvas. It remained in his personal possession until his death and it was auctioned in 1918.)

Degas' connections with the Impressionist group

During the years 1865–70 Degas exhibited regularly at the Salon but during this period his art underwent a transformation. The most obvious manifestation of this was his decision to give up history painting and turn to a new range of subject matter. This change of direction arose partly from his contacts with a new circle of acquaintances. His introduction to the Impressionists was through Manet, with whom for reasons of age and temperament he was apparently at ease. The English writer George Moore reported Manet as remarking on the ironic contrast between the subject matter of his own work and that of Degas at this time: 'When I was painting modern-life, Degas was still painting Semiramis'. (**Pl. II.25**, the subject of the painting was taken from an opera of that title.) The suggestion is that Degas responded later than Manet to the Baudelairean call for *'modernité'* in painting. As we have seen, Degas actively participated in the discussions at the Café Guerbois, where the generation of young artists gathered around Manet. Although differing from the Impressionists in class, education and perhaps temperament, he displayed sympathy for the group's subsequent attempt to exhibit and obtain public recognition. Among his contributions to the First Impressionist exhibition was the *Carriages at the Races* (**Col. pl.II.19**). (In Part 3, there will be a discussion of the critical response that his work received.)

Though Degas was as we have seen one of the most active organizers and most faithful supporters of the group's exhibitions over the period 1874–86, he preserved an independent position from the group as a whole. In a letter to the artist Tissot (*Supplementary Documents* II.1) he offered one reason for this: 'The realist movement no longer needs to fight with others. It is, it exists, it has to show itself *separately*; there must be a *Realist Salon.'*

Degas was not happy to accept the designation 'Impressionist' for their exhibitions, and in his notebooks of 1879 recorded his own suggestions for the Fourth Exhibition: either 'Exhibition by a group of independent artists', or 'by a group of realist and impressionist artists.' When Degas used the term 'realist' he meant to refer to those, such as Manet and his circle, whose interests were in portraying the contemporary world and the modern subject, rather than the worlds of history, myth and the Bible.

In the following sections we will be considering what aspects of contemporary life Degas represented, what view of his subjects his pictures reflected and what techniques he employed in making them, while in Part 3 we will consider what meanings these paintings had for Degas' contemporaries, and in that context assess the Modernist account of Impressionism and Degas.

Degas' techniques and technical interests

Degas' notebooks

During most of his working life, from 1853 to 1886 and possibly later, Degas kept notebooks. In these books Degas sketched or wrote down ideas for subjects, reminders of things seen, plans for future works, names and addresses of friends, aquaintances and models, and other tangential matters relating to his social life and activity as an artist (see **Pls.II.26–29**). The thirty-eight surviving notebooks contain over 2,500 pages, some of them unused. All the texts and many of the drawings contained in them, which range from doodles to more elaborate studies, have been scrupulously catalogued and reproduced in Theodore Reff's two-volume work, *The Notebooks of Edgar Degas* (1976). Notebook No. 18 (1859–64) is particularly interesting for its illustrations, which show Degas' early concern with contemporary life. They include fashionable crowds, a scene at the theatre, sailors fighting, prize fighters and spectators (in one, a hefty female boxer with gloves on is squared up against a male), the crowd in a public dance hall, carriages in the *Bois,* and travellers emerging from the Gare St Lazare.

In Notebook No. 23 (1868–72) Degas comments on physiognomic expression in both academic and modern style. He indicates his acquaintance with the work of Johann-Kaspar Lavater, a Swiss poet and theologian, whose *Physiognomic Fragments* appeared in 1775–78. Degas notes: 'make a *tête d'expression* [in academic parlance, a study of modern feeling]. It is a Lavater, but a Lavater more relative as it were, with accessory symbols at times' (Reff, *Notebooks,* No. 23, page 44). In the same notebook Degas records in writing his interest in the pictorial possibilities of the 'effects of light' from lamps and candles at night.

In Notebook No. 30 (1877–83) Degas makes a record of a bakers' establishment for a future project:

> At the baker's, *bread.* Series on *mitrons* seen in the cellar. [A *mitron* was the traditional paper cap used by bakers, like a bishop's mitre and sculpturally appealing.] Also a view across the ventilators leading to the street. Colour of flour, lovely curves of dough [*pâte*]. Still lifes on the different breads. Large, oval, fluted, round, etc. Experiments in colour, on the yellows, pinks, greys, whites of breads. Perspective views of rows of bread, ravishing layout of bakeries. Cakes, the wheat, the mills, the flour, the sacks, the market-porters.
>
> (Reff, *Notebooks,* No. 30, page 134)

In the same notebook are other proposals similar in genre: an artist's atelier, dancers in a variety of poses ('do a series of movements'), a hairdresser at work, and 'women's corsets being removed'. Here also Degas shows his interest in musicians at work and in the forms of the musical instruments themselves. He notes the possibility of funeral processions and crowds of carriages as subjects. He was also interested, as he indicates in this notebook, in doing studies in perspective and 'houses and monuments from below, close in; as one sees them when passing by on the street'. Of the various projects contemplated by Degas in this notebook, one of the most striking deals with variations on smoke:

. . . smoke from smokers, pipes, cigarettes, cigars, the smoke of locomotives, from high chimneys, factories, steamboats, etc., the piling up of smoke under the bridges, steam.

(Reff, *Notebooks*, No. 30)

The tendency of Modernist criticism is to consider an artist's techniques as the means by which expressive effects are achieved. But it is important to remember that to study an artist's techniques is to consider the resources employed in addressing the problems of subject matter and representation. We should not, therefore, discuss Degas' techniques simply as means to produce what *we* see in his work, but as means to understand what *he* saw, and saw as vivid, both in his own world and in the practice of art.

Degas as a technician

Theodore Reff devotes a whole chapter of *Degas: The Artist's Mind* (1976) to technique. He points out that Degas was both conservative, in that he continued to employ the conventional techniques of European art, and radical, in that he experimented constantly with new materials and methods.

Degas' training with Lamothe gave him the opportunity to study and to employ the conventional techniques preserved by the nineteenth-century studio tradition. He followed these methods in oil painting and drawing during the first years of his work; nor did he entirely abandon them later in his career. His early portrait of the Bellelli family **(Pl.II.30)** is conventional in technique and shows the oil paint applied in uniformly thin, flat strokes to give a smooth surface reminiscent of a painting by Ingres. But he did also experiment at the same time with a number of unusual procedures, particularly in the case of preparatory studies for his larger compositions. The study for the *Young Spartan Girls Provoking the Boys* is painted in oil on oiled paper which allows for easy and smooth application of the paint **(Pl.II.24)**. Later, by contrast, he employed a method which allowed him to achieve a dry, chalky effect. He would soak the oil out of the colours and dilute them with turpentine, hence the name *peinture à l'essence*. His painting *Racehorses at Longchamps* demonstrates the effect of this technique **(Col. pl.II.17)**.

In his use of pastel too, Degas attempted a variety of means to extend the pictorial possibilities of that medium. Pastel consists of powdered chalk and pigment mixed into a paste, which is then dried and held as one would hold a stick of charcoal. As you can see in *Dancers Resting* **(Pl.II.31)** it can be applied to the paper with a smooth or glossy finish in short and even strokes. Degas was able to see examples of eighteenth-century artists' pastels in his father's collection and in the collection of his father's friend, La Caze. It was in the 1870s that he really began to explore the possibilities of the medium. He would add it to a drawing which had been coloured with oils thinned in turpentine in order, for example, to give highlights to a dancer's costume (*The Rehearsal*, 1875, **Col. pl.II.20**). He began to use it in conjunction with prints, adding colour to these monochrome designs (*Café Concert*, **Col. pl.II.14**). Denis Rouart supplies the basic account of Degas' method. He describes how Degas invented a way of steaming his pastels to form a semi-liquid paste; he would then spread it with a brush, sometimes to form a wash. He used this to give an even tone to the background of his pictures and, as Rouart points out: 'He took great care not to spray the water vapour all over the picture, so as to give variety. He would not treat the flesh of the dancer in exactly the same way as her tutu, or the scenery might be given a different quality from the floor'. (Denis Rouart, *Degas à la Recherche de sa technique,* quoted by Dunlop, op. cit., 1979, page 170.)

Degas' notebooks also contain numerous recipes and ideas for technical projects

— especially those pertaining to print-making — with observations on appropriate chemical solutions and their effects on plate and print. A letter from Degas to Pissarro in 1880 provides additional evidence of Degas' keen interest in the technique of printmaking:

> Take a really smooth metal plate (this is essential, you understand). Remove every trace of grease with whiting. You have previously dissolved some resin in a strong concentration of alcohol. You pour this liquid, in the same way as photographers pour the collodion over their glass plates, taking care just as they do to tilt the plate and let it drain thoroughly; the liquid evaporates and leaves the plate covered with a layer of little grains of resin of varying thickness. When the plate is bitten, you are left with a grained effect that is dark or pale according to the depth of the bite. This is necessary if you want to obtain even tints. Less regular effects can be obtained by using a stump or the fingertip or any other form of pressure on the paper that is placed over the soft ground.
>
> (Dunlop, op.cit., 1979, page 171)

In his print of Mary Cassatt in the Louvre (Pl. II.32) Degas has combined the techniques of etching, aquatint, drypoint and *crayon électrique*. The various possibilities of these different print methods allowed him a great variety of tonal and linear rendering. Aquatint allows for the marbled effect on the wall and the grainy surface of the floor. The deep sooty black of the women's costume arises from allowing acid to bite deep into the plate which thus receives plenty of ink at the printing stage. The scratchy texture comes from using the pointed steel needle of the drypoint method together with the point of an electric filament, hence the term *crayon électrique*.

Particularly in Degas' monotypes, the variety of tone can be great. This medium lends itself well to experiment in tone and textured surface. A monotype, as the term implies, is a unique print taken from a drawing or painting made on a glass or metal plate or, for that matter, on any other receptive surface. Usually the medium is printer's ink or oil paint. Depending on the thickness and character of the medium on the plate, and the special effects sought, the print is taken either by means of a press or by some other means of putting pressure on the paper which receives the image.

That should indicate to you the scope this technique offers for variety in image-making. Merely dropping ink on one side of a sheet of paper, folding it over and rubbing it, produces what is in effect a monotype. If you've ever tried this you will know how striking some of the results can be, and how inviting for further elaboration. As Eugenia Janis observed in her account of Degas' monotypes:

> Degas could quickly create textures and half tones in the ink. He even began using his own fingerprints to grey the black and white contrasts. Large, broad shapes could be changed quickly and easily by adding or wiping away ink here or there at will. What is more, the artist could work at a leisurely pace. Making a monotype requires speed only in the printing because, once the paper has been dampened, the artist must go about transferring the ink to the paper with pressure quickly before the paper dries. The ink on the plate, consisting mostly of oil, does not dry quickly and can be worked over and over again by the artist before he prints. The greasy ink, slow to dry, and therefore always in a potential state of change on the plate, plus the occasional use of transparent celluloid plates (Degas could lift the plate and see his design in reverse as it would look when it was printed without stopping actually to print it) allowed Degas to keep the monotype sketch in a fleeting state for a longer period of time.
>
> (Eugenia Janis, *Degas' Monotypes*, 1968)

An examination of the background of Degas' monotype of the *Women Sitting in Front of a Café* (Col. pl. II.21) demonstrates the force of Janis' remarks on the advantages of the 'accidental' nature of this particular process for the artist's rendering of reflections in the glass of a café window.

▶ What conclusions would you draw from this brief account of the variety of Degas' techniques and of their relations to his subjects? ◀

▷ What does seem clear is that variety was important to him. He also seems to have been particularly concerned to exploit the suggestive possibilities of different media, each with its own textures and properties. I stressed at the outset of this section that the technical resources which an artist employs will tell us something about what he or she remarks and finds interesting. The conclusion seems to be that Degas was interested in those aspects of the world about him which particularly signified its variety, and also that he was concerned to equip himself with the means to respond to what was accidentally and fortuitously and *unpredictably* interesting. ◁

Degas and the Japanese print

There were two developments in the cultural life of Paris in the 1860s which appear to have had a direct influence on Degas' technical practice: the discovery of Japanese woodblock prints and the progress of photography. After the reopening of trade with Japan in 1854 the first prints made their way into Europe as wrapping papers. Two years later Degas' friend the engraver Felix Braquemond is reputed to have discovered a print by Hokusai in a packing case. Degas was one of the first to frequent the famous shop called La Porte Chinoise that Madame Desoiye opened under the arcades of the Rue de Rivoli in 1862. Following the success of the Oriental pavilions at the Expositions Universelles of 1867 and 1878, *japonaiserie* became fashionable and artists began to decorate their studios with Japanese prints and to pose their models in kimonos.

▶ Please compare the following plates:
UTAGAWA KUNIYOSHI, *View of the Post Stations* (Col. pl.III.15)
EDGAR DEGAS, *The Rehearsal* (Col. pl.II.20)

What compositional features do these two images have in common? ◀

▷ The two images share the compositional features of asymmetry, lack of a central focal point, looming foreground features (the tree trunks and the spiral staircase) and figures cut by the borders and brought close to the spectator in a direct and 'intimate' way. It seems that the Japanese print-maker's use of line and contour was a demonstration of the draughtsman's art to which Degas could respond, and which he adapted to his own use. Partly in response to the demands of the wood-block medium, the Japanese established a sense of space in pictorial form by silhouetting objects or people in the foreground against more distant landscape or domestic or decorative detail. This corresponds to certain forms of visual experience in real life. In the theatre for example, our view of the stage can be partially obstructed by a column, the spectator's head in front, or the musician in the orchestra pit. As you can observe in *The Orchestra at the Opéra* (Pl. II.33) Degas began to make use of these compositional devices towards the end of the 1860s. A comparison with Daumier's lithograph of 1852 showing the orchestra during a performance (Pl. II.34) provides a caution, however. Before the first imports of Japanese prints, Daumier had already seen the compositional and humorous potential of this particular subject. Therefore I should like to suggest that for Degas Japanese prints acted more as a confirmation that such compositional devices were pictorially sound, and potentially interesting, than as a source of entirely novel ideas. It is also perhaps relevant, however, that the technical qualities of Japanese prints were largely developed in the representation of scenes associated with the theatre, with everyday life, and with the Oriental equivalent of the demi-monde. Degas' interest in photography, as we shall see in the following section, can similarly be said to be both an interest in the validation of novel compositional devices and a confirmation of the cultural currency of certain subjects. ◁

Photography

In considering the impact of photography on Degas it is useful at this stage briefly to estimate the impact photography had on art in general in the nineteenth century. Photography offered a new source of pictorial imagery of a range unimaginable in previous centuries. It could not be ignored. In one way or another, all artists in the later nineteenth century worked under 'the shadow of the lens'. To many artists and critics the camera appeared as the nemesis of painting. Its development and its greatest impact coincided with, and was almost certainly of relevance to, the development of certain preoccupations which are singled out in Modernist history. In particular it offered apparent solutions and technical shortcuts to contemporary pictorial problems, and thus seemed to pose an ultimate threat to art's traditional representational function: that of capturing likenesses.

Both Courbet and Manet made occasional use of photographs – as you saw in Block I, Figure 5 (page 14) Courbet may have used photographs as a direct source. The Impressionists (particularly Monet), who were concerned with a kind of naturalistic accuracy in which a high priority was accorded to effects of light, could hardly ignore a medium which not only appeared to cater to the same interests, but also offered to automate the processes by which those interests might be satisfied.

Figure 4   Photograph of a Paris boulevard c. 1860, by Ferrier and Solier. Courtesy, International Museum of Photography at George Eastman House, Rochester, New York.

But Degas was the only artist of his era to see qualities in photographic imagery which, though distinct from those of artistic pictures, might be exploited and incorporated in his own representational activity. Those very aspects which photographers of the time rejected as accidents or 'aberrations' in their medium were perceived by Degas as suggestions for new ways of composing pictures. But before we can establish the extent to which Degas' use of photography was innovative and experimental, we need to look at the ways in which photography was received and exploited by some of his contemporaries.

From its introduction in 1839 till the end of the century, artists and critics alike were divided in their opinions about the effect of photography on art. It was seen both as a curse and a blessing. Would photography make painting redundant, or would it improve its efficiency by showing fastidious draughtsmen the way to greater accuracy in pictorial representation? Plainly the importance accorded to such issues would depend on the extent to which the essential function of painting was identified with the production of likenesses. The development of photography must have played its part in generating that typically modern defence of the artist's function which emerged in the later nineteenth century: not so much to imitate and to reproduce, as to 'express' and to 'create'.

At first the reception of photography was more enthusiastic than not. It would become an indispensable aid to the artist:

> . . . the daguerreotype does not deprive the landscape painter of his bread and butter; on the contrary he can make it yield profitable returns. He can photograph a locality with the daguerreotype in a few minutes, to serve as a sketch for painting in any desired proportions at home.
>
> (*Gazette de France.*)

The equation of time with money is readily apparent in that and other early reports on photography's application to art. The utilitarian value of photography was foremost in the entrepreneurial mind and within the commercial ambience of nineteenth-century Europe and America. Enthusiasm was expressed for the 'variety beyond expectation' which photography would discover in the hidden minutiae of nature (Fox Talbot, 1844).

But far from providing facility and detail in the reproduction of natural appearances, as some had imagined it would, photography quickly became a trap for guileless artists. In the attempt to compete with its 'realistic' effects, veracity and skilful execution became *de rigueur* and often even an obsession for the less technically inventive painters. The dangers inherent in photography were realized by Baudelaire as early as 1859. In photography, the 'demon of progress', he saw the death of true art. It would be all the more disastrous for having come to the fore at a time of obsessive preoccupation with 'nature'. Instead of searching for 'Beauty' in art, the public were now fixated upon 'Truth', and to satisfy this demand artists were neglecting what had traditionally been important aspects of their own professional domain – the spiritual, the imaginary, the subjective – in favour of banal and trivial aspects of nature. Thus under the influence of photography, Baudelaire claimed, the quality of art had already suffered and would continue to suffer a marked decline. This implied criticism of the importance accorded to descriptive 'finish' in art was consistent with the production by the Impressionists of 'sketchy' pictures as paintings in themselves.

Other critics pointed out the dangers of the abuse of photography. The influential Théophile Gautier, for example, wrote in 1861 of the *trompe-l'oeil* effects, the photographic exactitude and extreme realism which marked a preponderance of paintings shown that year at the Salon. Facetiously scathing, he described the paintings of Charles Nègre, equally well-known as a photographer of Parisian life. Nègre was an artist who based a number of his paintings on his own photographs

(Pls.II.35,36). His photographs, if not his paintings, are today held in high esteem. Gautier singled our several other painters in the same way:

> . . . one can guess from the crispness of the details, from the mathematically correct placing of the shadows, that he has taken the daguerreotype as a collaborator. The daguerreotype, which has not been named and which hasn't received any medal, has none the less done much work at the exhibition. It has provided plenty of information, spared many models from posing, furnished lots of accessories — settings and draperies — so that all that was necessary was to copy them in colour.
>
> (Abécédaire du Salon de 1861)

(The 'daguerreotype' had in fact by 1861 been superseded by other photographic processes, but the term was used generically at the time to denote all kinds of photography.)

Three years later, the painter Paul Huet, friend of Delacroix and a colourist in the Romantic manner, warned artists of the threat from 'the machine':

> The daguerreotype has troubled a lot of heads: nothing is more false nor more dangerous than the extreme perfection of this instrument. It can be used for reference where a detail is concerned, but one ought to guard against allowing oneself to be seduced by this impossible rendering, this false perspective. One should pass the magnifying glass over to science; the eyes are sufficient to appreciate the beauties of the landscape. There is something in an artist's work which no instrument can give.
>
> (On Painting after Nature, 1864)

Several issues are raised by this short quotation from Huet. It may help to explain some of the more sympathetic early responses to Impressionist painting. And we might keep in mind his reference, especially, to the 'false perspective' of the photograph, a warning also given by Delacroix and others. This factor is significant in our consideration of Degas' compositional means.

A merely descriptive 'realism', with which photographic realism was equated, was seen increasingly by those with 'modern' sympathies as the antithesis of art. The derogatory term 'daguerreotype' even came to be used against writers with an inordinate fondness for descriptive accuracy. So long as 'truth' remained the principal criterion for artistic competence, as it did in academic circles for most of the latter part of the century, and so long as 'truth' was equated with descriptive likeness, photographic art was bound to be rated highly, and more individual and expressive interpretations of nature were bound to be judged as aberrant and wilful distortions. For the many critics whose notions of artistic achievement and truth to nature had been formed by their experience of Salon art, the paintings of the Impressionists, with their bold colours and undisguised brushwork, appeared even more indefensible than they might have done before the development of photography. But although Impressionist painting was markedly different from photographic imagery and form, it could still be presented as fundamentally compatible with naturalism (once the initial hostility to technical novelty had been overcome). It took a change of aesthetic values, in particular the attack upon realism mounted by the Symbolists in the 1880s, and the demand for an art that was more interpretative than mimetic, finally to turn the tables against photographic art.

It was perhaps as a result of this change in aesthetics that even Degas' imaginative techniques, which could actually be seen as subverting, rather than supporting, the valuation of photographic techniques, came towards the end of his career to be considered too 'photographic' by some commentators. This may also account in some degree for the artist's stubborn refusal to admit of any influence at all from photography. Indeed, right after Degas' death in 1917, his old friend the painter Jacques-Émile Blanche tried to defend him against glib accusations that his style was merely photographic.

His system of composition was new . . . no one before Degas ever thought of doing them, no one since has put such 'gravity' into the kind of composition which utilizes to advantage the accidents of the camera.

(*De David à Degas,* 1919, pages 297–8.)

▶ The 'accidents of the camera' is a key term in any consideration of Degas' use of the photographic image. I would like you now to compare Degas' *The Rehearsal of the Ballet on Stage,* 1873 (**Col. pl.II.15**) with a photograph of about the same date, *The Foyer of the Opéra* (**Pl. II.37**).

First describe the compositional differences between them and comment on their visible expressive features. Then, try to estimate what both Degas and the photographer might have been aiming for in the organization of their subjects by comparing them to an example of a conventional academic composition (**Col. pl.I.5**). ◀

▷ Despite the fact that, strictly speaking, the subjects are not parallel in setting, a number of points can be made. Although both seem designed to establish an overall impression of informality, as suggested, for instance, by figures arrested in action, both painter and photographer have carefully organized the elements of their compositions, albeit differently and with different effects.

In the photograph, the dancers and their 'admirers' are crowded, with little to relieve the spatial compression, while in the painting the figures are arranged singly, or in groups to produce a representation of spatial volume and openness, and a sense of the possibility of movement into depth.

To enhance the impression of space and movement, Degas established a viewpoint close to the foreground figures. Indeed, we seem so close that we only see the looming scrolls of two 'cellos which in size are almost equal to the dancers right of centre, only about fifteen or twenty feet further back. Conversely, the lateral row of dancers in the photograph not only impedes our view into the picture space, but because the camera's position is well back from these figures in the foreground, the perspective is less exaggerated and the picture space seems shallower. It seems that one of the photographer's means for producing an impression of progression into depth is to place the seated male figure in the angle made by the foreground dancer's arms. This looks contrived. No such thing occurs in the Degas. Though we know that all the compositional elements must have been carefully calculated and contrived, apparent accidents abound of a kind that we now associate with the casual snapshot photograph: the odd position of the girl's arm at the left, as she holds on to the scenery flat; the ambiguity in the upper limbs of the clutch of dancers right of centre (how many are there?); the curious way in which the dancing master's hand seems to touch that of the dancer in the distance, and more of the kind. Very little pictorial imagination is shown in the photograph, despite its obvious 'staging'.

One final comment (though these works would support much additional analysis in terms of pose, expression and gesture for example): Degas' figures are cut off by the frame, and, even within the picture, by the stage prop at the left. Consider also the three dancers behind the prop. Nothing of the kind is seen in the photograph, where all is neatly posed around a central axis. The dancer in the left foreground of the photograph faces inwards; the woman in the crinoline, right background, also. The whole composition is frontal, perpendicular with the frame, unlike the oblique view of the painting. That in itself is not a weakness, except in so far as it would have been incompatible with any aim of the photographer artificially to convey a measure of spontaneity in a 'fortuitous' view.

On the question of what Degas and the photographer might have had in mind when producing these pictures, it seems probable that the photographer, far from trying to establish a new compositional type, had a conventional kind of painterly composition in mind, while Degas seems to have employed characteristics which might be found in those types of photographs which might then have been regarded as incompetent. In terms of subject matter, notice also the mild sexual implication of the photographic scene, for it parallels in some degree the conception of the laundress in nineteenth-century France which we will come to later in the block. ◁

So it was not what were normally seen as the competent technical qualities of photography which lent impetus to Degas' search for modern means to convey modern subjects. It was rather the 'unacceptable' aspects, the technical 'mistakes' and the shortcomings of the photographic image which caught his attention. These photographic 'faults' — the gross tonal contrasts, figures cut by the frame, exaggerated scale of perspective, the crude and unexpected positions in which figures are captured in some awkward phase of movement, unusual viewpoints and angles — were all distinctive consequences of the photographic process.

A further confirmation of Degas' use of photographs was provided recently when, in 1976, the Bibliothèque Nationale in Paris made prints from three positive glass plates discovered in their collection of Degas material. The subject is a dancer (or possibly three dancers) in three different poses (Pls. II.38–43). Some evidence suggests that the photographs were made in the 1870s, though this is not proven. Buerger (1978) proposes that the plates, though they are positive images, were used by Degas to obtain prints from which he studied the strange negative and other reversal effects produced in these particular images. This certainly is consistent with Degas' readiness to induce, and experiment with, all manner of accidental effects in any graphic medium and to explore that medium for a wide range of expressive possibilities. And here, particularly, the three poses of the dancer and the peculiarities of tone appear together in Degas' pastel drawing of c.1897, *Four Dancers* (**Pl. II.44**) and, with variations, in many other paintings and pastel drawings made between 1896 and 1899 (**Pl. II.45** especially). You can see for yourself in the illustrations here the kind of luminous, sculptural effects Degas derived from these evocative photographs — particularly by consulting a positive 'contretype' as it appears in one of the glass plates (**Pl. II.40**).

As Buerger with good reason points out, by exploiting a wide range of possible variations and combinations, Degas was able to derive from these three photographs material for 'over one hundred drawings and pastels that he executed in or around 1897 and the following years' (J. Buerger, *Image,* 1978, Vol. 2). A curious letter from Degas to an artist friend, written probably in the early 1880s, offers support to the view that he found photographs useful. Degas asks for a pass to the Opéra: 'I have done so many of these dance examinations *without* having seen them [my emphasis] that I'm a bit ashamed of it' (Marcel Guérin (ed.) *Lettres de Degas*, 1945, Letter No. XXIII).

Now, what does this statement tell us about Degas' method of working? I think it suggests that he stuck close to his studio, that his earlier sketches and other reference material (such as the three photographs of a dancer) provided him with the basic ingredients for a wide range of permutations. Out of such restricted resources he could produce a great number of compositional variations on only a few themes. Degas no doubt knew, from his study of earlier artists, the way in which they worked over a single motif in different ways, reusing figures in different positions and combinations. Of course, we are talking here about what Degas did in the studio. Outside the studio he appears to have kept his eyes open. The resources of the studio enabled him to represent and revise what he noticed and remembered at the Opéra, at the ballet, at the races, on the streets of Paris, and in brothels, laundries, cafés and the houses of friends.

Some typical themes in Degas' work

In the previous sections we have seen that both formal and technical characteristics in Degas' pictures have a representational function. They represent ways of showing the *subject* to the spectator and of showing it in terms of specific aspects and interests.

For the following discussion, it will be helpful if you arrange your Degas illustrations in roughly chronological order. Although your illustrations only represent a small selection of Degas' work, several general points can be made on the nature and choice of his subject matter over his working career. We can see that his early work is split largely between portraiture and history painting. Portraiture continued to be a concern until his later years, but in the second half of the 1860s, the time when Monet and Renoir worked at La Grenouillère, he gave up history painting altogether. The influence of Manet and through him of Baudelaire and of Zola is often cited. You have already considered in Block I (pages 26ff) Baudelaire's contribution in providing a theoretical and artistic basis for the celebration of a novel species of subject matter dealing with contemporary themes (see also Radiovision programme 3).

Although Baudelaire's evocations of Paris obliquely refer to Constantin Guys, some of Degas' later themes seem remarkably close to Baudelaire's descriptions. No reference to Baudelaire is known from Degas' surviving letters but Manet wrote to Degas in 1869 asking him to return the two Baudelaire books he had borrowed. Theodore Reff (1976, page 150) suggests with good reason that the books were *Curiosités esthétiques* (1865) and *L'Art Romantique* (1869).

We know from notes written in Degas' earlier notebooks, especially those beginning in 1863 (the year that Baudelaire's *Painters of Modern Life* first appeared in *Le Figaro*) that the young Degas, notwithstanding his current production of paintings based on conventional historical themes, had an eye to subjects which sprang both from private and public occurrences in contemporary life. This type of entry continues in his later notes (about 1869–72 and thereafter) defining a range of scenes, subjects, details and themes for the depiction of contemporary urban life. His paintings and drawings of the 1870s show an increased interest in urban life in nineteenth-century Paris. He studied the racecourse (**Pl. II.46**) the stock exchange (**Pl. III.4**), the ballet, the orchestra pit, laundries (**Pl. II.47**), brothels (Radiovision programme 4) and the *Café Concert* (**Col. pl. II.14**). The latter were initially places of entertainment catering mainly for the working class. At first they consisted simply of a small stage erected at one end of a café, but in time they became more elaborate and attracted a richer class of clientèle. The management of the cafés tried to employ as many pretty singers as possible. In 1870 an American visitor noted:

> The object of the management seems to be to keep as many of them as possible constantly before the gaze of the audience, and as soon as the performer is through with her part, she returns to her seat on the stage . . . . You notice that all of the women have bouquets – they are gifts of the admirers of the 'artistes'. A person wishing to make the acquaintance of one of these fair demoiselles, sends a bouquet with his card to her. If she appears with it on the stage, she thereby signifies her willingness to accept Monsieur's attentions.
>
> (James D. McCabe Jr., *Paris by Sunlight and Gaslight,* 1870, quoted in Dunlop, 1979, page 151.)

In Degas' depiction of one of the café concerts we see a singer holding a bouquet, presumably a gift from an admirer, while others lean over the footlights to capture the attention of their audience.

Contemporary reviews of Degas' work in the 1870s tended to emphasize his role as a 'painter of modern life'. 'The totality [of his works] constitutes an incomparable page from the contemporary story-book' ('Jacques', *Homme Libre,* 12 April 1877).

In the 1880s Degas appears more preoccupied with the female nude, though not the classicist nude of academic art. His drawings and paintings at that time show women absorbed in the intimate tasks of bathing, drying and combing their hair and dressing (**Pl. II.48,** *The Tub*). He exhibited ten pastels of female nude subjects at the last Impressionist exhibition in 1886 (see **Pl. II.49** and Hamilton, pages 22–3).

What are we to make of this catalogue of Degas' subject matter? We could sum it up by stating that Degas was interested in representing modern life and then ask why. But there are more interesting questions to ask about the particular nature and choice of Degas' subject matter. What aspects of contemporary life did he represent? What type of view on contemporary life is represented in his pictures, and how did his techniques serve to express it? What would have been the impact of exhibiting such representations? What meanings would they have had for the contemporary spectator? One contemporary reaction to Degas' representation of modern life was given by the novelist and critic, Edmond de Goncourt:

> Yesterday I spent the afternoon in the studio of a painter named Degas. After many attempts, many bearings taken in every direction, he has fallen in love with the modern and, in the modern, he has cast his eyes upon laundresses and dancers. I cannot find his choice bad, since I, in [my novel] *Manette Salomon*, have spoken of these two professions as ones that provide for a modern artist the most picturesque models of women in this time . . .
>
> He is the man I have seen up to now who has best captured, in reproducing modern life, the soul of this life.
>
> (*Journal*, 13 February 1874, quoted in Rewald, 1973, pages 278–9)

When Goncourt says that laundresses and dancers are 'picturesque' he probably means 'worthy to be pictured' rather than pretty or quaint. If these two professions, which were then both exclusively *female* professions, were taken to represent modern life they must have had a peculiar significance for Goncourt and his contemporaries which is lost to us today.

Ballet dancers

► Take out **Col. pls. II.**15,16,20, and **Pls. II.**31,44,45 and 50–53. These show a selection of the studies of ballet scenes which preoccupied Degas during the 1870s. Lay them out on a flat surface where you can compare them easily. ◄

These scenes of ballet dancers are the ones that we tend readily to associate with Degas. The enormous surviving number of paintings and drawings on this theme bears witness to his fascination with the subject of these young girls and with the type of work in which they were involved. According to Lilian Browse (1949) who made a special study of Degas' dancers, these little *rats* of the ballet came from poor homes, entered the Opéra between the ages of seven and eight, and grew up with little or no education. At ten, if they showed promise, they were given a salary of nine hundred francs a year, a fortune for many of the girls. They then spent eight to nine years taking classes and preparing to become members of the chorus. Theodore Reff (1978) has plausibly suggested that one of the reasons why Degas was so interested in the dancers was that their long arduous training and rehearsals corresponded to the hours of effort that Degas believed the artist should spend drawing and studying.

During the summer of 1872 Degas gained access to the practice rooms of the Paris Opéra and was able to observe the ballet master and choreographer, Louis François Mérante, conducting a class. As a result of these visits Degas painted two small-scale oil paintings. **Pl. II.50** shows one of these, the painting which Degas was able to sell at Durand-Ruel's gallery in London in the year that it was painted. A dancing class is shown in progress with one dancer posed ready to begin her steps. In comparison to the later studies that you have, it appears that Degas was not prepared, at this stage, to show dancers in motion. The remaining illustrations show a selection of the series of related pictures which Degas worked on after his return to Paris in 1873 from a visit to his relatives in New Orleans. *The Dance Class* **(Pl.II.53)** is related to a study of the famous dancer, Mlle Gaujelin, who modelled for Degas. Many of these studies of dancers exist in two or three versions (**Col. pls. II.15,16**).

From 1875 onwards Degas concentrated on showing the effects on his subjects of the long hours of training and exercise. In his depiction of the dancers he seems to have recognized the mental concentration which was required for dancing and the gruelling physical effort which left them slumped on benches once they had finished their exercises (**Pl. II.31**, pastel). As a comparison of the two oil paintings of dance classes will confirm (**Pl. II.50**, 1872, and **Col. pl. II.20**, *c.* 1875) the later studies show a greater interest in movement and in more complex lighting, as for example the effect of backlighting on the dancers performing arabesques in the background in your colour illustration.

▶ Please compare two versions of *The Rehearsal of the Ballet on Stage* (**Col. pls. II.15, II.16**) in terms of composition and use of media, noting how these affect what we see in the two scenes. (Note that the media used for **Col. pl. II.15** included not only oil mixed with turpentine, but also watercolour and pastel over a pen and ink drawing.) ◀

▷ Firstly it is essential to note what these images describe. We see what appears to be a ballet rehearsal taking place on a theatre stage. There are indications of the ornate architecture characteristic of theatres at that time, scenery and the heads of 'cellos looming in the foreground. The ballet master directs a group of dancers centre stage, other dancers await their turn. Two seated gentlemen appear on the far side of the stage (possibly admiring their favourite, or awaiting the opportunity for some sexually-motivated patronage). Both designs show compositional features that we have noticed previously in Degas' work. They both show an unexpected angle of vision, cut-off forms, abrupt contrast of scale in the figures and objects depicted, all combining to give a powerful suggestion of the way a spectator might actually experience the sight of a ballet rehearsal. (And it is consistent with the majority of Degas' later works, as we shall see, that a complex relationship is maintained between the 'aesthetic' of spectatorship, and voyeurism. You may recall that the complexity of this relationship had already been rendered art-historically vivid by Manet.) The system of highlights on the right-hand side of the stage and on the dancers' costumes imply that the scene is taking place under the artificial glare of footlights. The mixed media with their smudgy effects and brightly coloured accents enhance the impression of figures and objects lit by the peculiar reflective qualities of this type of light.

This said, there are compositional and technical differences between the two designs. The composition of the oil painting appears to have been worked on at greater length. There are more dancers depicted both performing and waiting in the wings. The seated dancer in the foreground is more securely located on a bench. By contrast, the composition of the pastel appears to benefit from various inventive forms of simplification. The two scroll heads of the 'cellos have been reduced to one strong diagonal accent placed at the lower left-hand corner. This decision allows the seated ballet dancer to be shown to maximum advantage.

Two girls only now wait in the wings and the same goes for the number of girls shown in the act of dancing on the stage. The two onlookers are shown in sharper relief. (It is interesting in this respect to note that the spectator's eye-level on the scene appears to coincide with the eye-level of these men, a pictorial conceit much enjoyed by Renaissance artists.) The result of Degas' use of a variety of media on the first design is that the tonal variations are more subtle and less clearly contrasted than in the pastel. The pastel shows much brighter tonal contrasts and intriguing colour effects. It is interesting to note the accents of bright blues and reds which serve to pull the background and foreground together into a coherent design.

In our view the pastel is more interesting and coherently worked out in terms of composition and media. There is, however, a danger in attaching too much significance to the comparative dating of the two works. At this stage Degas was constantly reworking his paintings, and it is extremely difficult to be confident about when he began and completed a work. Nevertheless this comparison should serve to demonstrate that Degas was both economic in his use of figures and compositions, and inventive in the revisions and improvisations which he practised on them.

The portraits

Throughout his working life Degas painted portraits. He had a remarkable gift for representing character as much through the posture as through the facial expression of his sitters. He himself is reported as saying, 'Be sure to give the same expression to a person's face that you give to his body. If laughter is a characteristic of a person, make him laughing' (Holt, 1966, page 403). It is interesting in this context to note the statements on portraiture made by Degas' friend, the novelist Edmond Duranty, in his defence of the Impressionists, in 'The New Painting' (1876):

> By means of a back, we want a temperament, an age, a social condition to be revealed; through a pair of hands, we should be able to express a magistrate or a tradesman; by a gesture, a whole series of feelings. A physiognomy will tell us that this fellow is certainly an orderly, dry, meticulous man, whereas that one is carelessness and disorderliness itself. An attitude will tell us that this person is going to a business meeting, whereas that one is returning from a love tryst. 'A man opens a door; he enters; that is enough; we see that he has lost his daughter.' Hands that are kept in pockets can be eloquent. The pencil will be steeped in the marrow of life.
>
> (Dunlop, 1979, page 165)

▶ Please take out the following plates:

The Bellelli Family, 1860–62 (**Pl. II.30**)
Place de la Concorde (*The Viscomte Lépic and his daughters*), 1875 (**Pl. II.54**)

Before doing the following exercise it would be helpful to know who the subjects are and how they were related to Degas.

The Bellelli Family   Degas' Aunt Laura was married to a Neapolitan, the Baron Bellelli. The marriage was apparently not a happy one. Degas' uncle wrote of it 'Incompatibility of personality and background and as a result a lack of affection and leniency enlarges like a magnifying glass the individuals' natural faults.' (Dunlop, page 41). The framed drawing on the back wall of the portrait has been identified by Theodore Reff (page 96) as a portrait of Degas' grandfather. The picture has therefore the function of a commemorative portrait and this explains why the women are wearing mourning. On his visit to Italy as a young man Degas visited his aunt and executed a series of drawings and portrait studies which he combined into this early group portrait of his relatives.

The Viscomte Lépic   The Viscomte was a friend of Degas with whom he collaborated on his first monotype. Lépic had many interests: he was an anthropologist, a dog-breeder and an engraver who took a particular interest in the technicalities of this craft. In 1876 he published a book of his experiments outlining different ways of inking plates. He was father to two spirited daughters and Degas painted the portrait of the father with his daughters and one of his hounds, crossing the Place de la Concorde.

How are expression and character indicated and expressed in each of these pictures? ◀

▷ In each of these portraits Degas seems to have caught the psychology of his subjects and, in the case of the early portrait, the individuals' feelings towards each other. Moreover, in the later portrait Degas demonstrates his gift for finding unexpected angles and situations which further direct attention to the character of his subjects.

Laura Bellelli stares with an impenetrable expression into space. The Baron is isolated, his awkward pose seems to suggest his tension and alienation from the other members of his family. The differentiation of the little girls' pose and glance suggests divided loyalties to the parents. The group as a whole is organized in a rather formal way. The figures are placed parallel to the surface of the picture. The setting around them is organized into a stable pattern of horizontal and vertical accents. The portrait still belongs to an earlier tradition of the ceremonial family portrait.

In the Lépic portrait Degas employs a decided cropping effect which suggests an unexpected and casual encounter with the group on the street. The three members of the Lépic family are caught in fractional part-movement. They have moved and will move again. There is a variety in the orientation between the father and his daughters. The portrait belongs as much to the series of Parisian street scenes painted by Manet, Monet, Renoir, Pissarro and Caillebotte as to portraiture (see **Pl. II.55**, Caillebotte's scene on the Pont de l'Europe). This is surely one of those paintings in which Degas referred to and exploited the 'cropping' effects and 'accidental' spatial qualities of the informal photograph. ◁

Figure 5   Photograph of Degas and friends in the rue de Rougement, Paris, 25 or 26 July 1889, by Count Guiseppe Primoli. Courtesy, Fondazione Primoli, Rome. (Degas is standing on the lady's right, in the straw hat.)

Contemporary meanings of Degas' subjects: laundresses

So far in this case study we have considered aspects of Degas' social background, his training, techniques, sources and some themes, but we have not yet attempted, as in Block I with Manet, a reconstruction of the contemporary meanings of Degas' paintings.

In the case study in Block I, Manet's paintings were explained in terms of their contemporary references and meanings. Manet's concern with ways of representing subjects and themes, ranging from low-life to public events, was shared by Degas. It is, therefore, our contention that a similar approach to the explanation of Degas' paintings is the most historically informative.

Also, as is established by Hollis Clayson in Radiovision programme 4, *Images of Prostitution*, it is historically uninformative to look at the representation of women without examining both existing representations and social and cultural 'discourses' on the status, and attitudes towards, the types of women represented. In Block I, you saw in Tim Clark's article on Manet's *Olympia* (Reader, Text 40) and his television programme, an approach which attempts to reconstruct the conditions in which works of art are produced and out of which specific social and cultural meanings are established. We do not wish to claim that such approaches are necessarily preferable to those which characterize Modernist methods for uncovering meaning in art. The point is rather that they yield different types of interpretation and therefore open the works up to speculation and argument.

▶ For these reasons, therefore, we want you now to read Eunice Lipton's article, 'The Laundress in Late Nineteenth-century French Culture: Imagery, Ideology and Edgar Degas', an edited version of which is in the Reader, Text 41. Please look at **Col. pl. II.22** and **Pls II.56 – 62**, which she discusses. Again, you should read this article as an explanation – a piece of historical research which has underlying assumptions and interests. In the light of information provided in this block so far, you may have things to criticize in her account. However, you should bear two questions in mind: what aspect of Degas' paintings is she interested in (she is obviously not trying to explain everything), and what information – sources, references etc., does she emphasize? ◀

▷ Firstly, the author *doesn't* assume that she can explain what laundresses meant to Degas by just examining Degas' work. She insists on reminding us that Degas lived in a society in which there were certain commonly accepted assumptions and prejudices, about the figure of the laundress, and that Degas could not have been unaware of these assumptions and prejudices, whether or not he shared them. He would certainly have been aware that his own representations would be approached by people who expected to see their assumptions and prejudices reflected in his work. This awareness would surely have affected his choice about what to emphasize or play down.

Secondly, Lipton draws attention to the existence of a *tradition of representations* of laundresses in both painting and literature. She comments on the frequency with which *blanchisseuses* were represented in France, not only in popular illustrated journals (Plates N and O in the Reader) but in literature, in the Salon exhibitions (**Pl. II.56**), and in mildly pornographic photographs (Plate P in the Reader). The erotic significance attached to laundresses (both washers and ironers, but ironers especially) had partly to do with their visibility and the steamy, sweaty atmospheres generated in their place of work, which made it necessary for them to wear light clothing. 'In Joseph Caraud's *Soubrette Repassant* (Salon, 1872) we gaze into a private domestic interior hung with intimate apparel.' While the maid is absorbed in her task, we are made the voyeurs of her décolletage (Pl. II.56). Lipton's case – and it is a strong one – is that these working women were regarded as little more than objects for sexual titillation. A contributing factor, as other writers have also observed, was that these women, ironers especially, were in a sense on display. The shop-fronts (usually with living quarters behind) were often glassed-in rather than boarded, and the doors left open for air. Moreover, such laundries were ubiquitous. The industry occupied (by Lipton's estimate) the surprising figure of one-fifth to one-third of the population of Paris and its suburbs. The long hours, poor pay and unhealthy conditions of the *blanchisseuses* no doubt contributed to the numbers of laundresses who were also prostitutes. (See also the table in Block I, page 46.)

Degas' many representations of ironers and washerwomen (twenty-seven or twenty-eight, excluding the sketches in his notebooks, according to Lipton) are seen as 'extraordinary'. According to Lipton, some of them, like the 'Munich' *Ironer* (Pl. II.59), express a kind of covert sexuality, a shyness due to Degas' probable celibacy and awkwardness in relations with the opposite sex. Intriguing evidence is advanced, some of it Freudian, to account for the artist's 'oblique' handling of this subject. The historical evidence Lipton advances to support this assertion is rather slender. We have to accept that we cannot recover reliable knowledge about Degas' psychology. On firmer ground is the suggestion that several works by Degas depicting laundresses are executed with an acute understanding of what such backbreaking work entails in bodily effort:

> Through a delimited and explicitly vocational repertory of gestures, Degas captures the ritualistic nature of ironing and forces us to see it. He does not, as the Degas literature would have us believe, merely wrap the women in a hazy glow of palpable light, nor is he simply fascinated with motion. Rather his drawing and spatial constructions reveal the women's solitude, their withdrawal, their fatigue. And when for a moment we are no longer only mesmerized by the magical light and brilliant drawing, we may be shocked to find ourselves face-to-face with the boredom and alienation inherent in such labour.

(Reader, page 282) ◁

Lipton's article offers what seems a legitimate form of inquiry into the sociological and ideological implications of Degas' imagery. She presents a defensible interpretation of what the figure of the laundress signified to Parisian society at that time. In the next part of the block you will be reading contemporary critical reactions to Degas' work and to that of his fellow Impressionists and considering whether their work was criticized on the grounds that what was represented was unacceptable, or because it was seen as technically incompetent, or both.

Having considered Degas' professional activities and his resulting work you may be surprised by some of the views expressed. As Eunice Lipton has demonstrated, it is necessary to consider public and professional concepts of art and its proper functions as among the determining conditions under which 'modern art' was produced.

One last point we should bear in mind, given the Modernist tendency to consider pictorial effects at the expense of representational functions. I'd suggest that in modern art generally, and in the work of the Impressionists and of Degas very specifically, novelty of representational technique is often just what alerts us to the need to take an inquiring attitude to *what* is represented. One thing that distinguishes the things we call works of art is that they are intended to have a certain appearance. It is through what is different and specific in their appearance that they gain our interest, including our interest in *what* is represented.

3 Impressionism and Degas: contemporary and subsequent criticism

It is impossible to understand an artist without coming to terms with his or her reputation. On the one hand, the reputation may be well-deserved, and thus may have much to teach us. One the other, it may be distorted, in which case it is likely that much has filtered through from these distorted views into supposedly 'objective' accounts of what the painter in question actually did, under what circumstances and, most tendentiously of all, why. Thirdly, a reputation gained during an artist's lifetime can influence the work he or she later does, especially when those who construct that reputation, the critics and historians, have influence on the painter's markets and thus on the painter's livelihood. Indeed, this may well affect not only how an artist subsequently works, but also his or her own retrospective accounts of what he or she was doing in earlier work. (This is a particular danger where an artist possesses a large number of unsold earlier works which he or she needs to sell to live.)

In this section we need to look at the reputations of Degas on the one hand and Monet, Renoir, Pissarro and Sisley on the other. The latter are of interest in their own right. To repeat; this group is often portrayed as the first avant-garde group within Modernist history. We need to touch on the question of how just these four have come to be singled out and treated in this special way. But we also need to look at their reputations if we are to gain an understanding of the critical writings relating to Degas. As we saw in Part 1, he and they brought their works together in a self-conscious attempt at creating a group identity of some sort in 1874, in the first exhibition of the *Societé anonyme des artistes, peintres, sculpteurs, graveurs etc.* – the 'First Impressionist Exhibition'.

The critical writings we shall examine relate principally to various of the shows in the series of similar exhibitions held over the next decade or so. Now as you will see from the Appendix, a great many artists other than the five we have been discussing contributed to these shows at one time or another, most of them contributing to some only, not all of these shows. And there was, as I shall explain, an intricate web of political considerations (I'm referring to the politics of the art world, but also, tangentially, to national politics) relating to the question of who exhibited with whom, when, and how often. The critical writings must be seen against the background of these considerations. It is arguable that in some cases these very writings were themselves part of the politics of the 'movement' – if indeed we may speak of a movement. Understanding what was written about Degas involves understanding what was written about other important contributors. It may be wondered whether Degas would have been received in the same way had he stayed out of these shows, as Manet did.

The First Impressionist Exhibition

In order to gain a clear picture of what the show was intended to be, what it actually was, and hence how one might have expected critics to react, we have to consider who actually exhibited, and what (and who refused to participate). First and importantly, we must be careful about whom we count as members of the 'core group'. Certainly this included Monet, Pissarro, Renoir and Sisley (who, with Morisot, deserves more attention than we have given him) and Degas. But there were also Cézanne, Guillaumin, Boudin, as well as others now no longer much remembered.

The important point is to beware the assumption that the central figures of the *Société anonyme* can be wrapped up in the formula, 'The four big Impressionists, plus Degas'. It is a significant historical question to ask why those four have been singled out and grouped together so often and whether Degas is rightly presented as some kind of anomaly. The way in which Cézanne is so often treated as a Post-Impressionist before his time, rather than a 'hard-core' Impressionist of the period, demonstrates that the persistence of this selection in the critical literature cannot be explained simply by saying, 'These were the most significant painters at the exhibition'.

We should also bear in mind those who were invited to join the exhibition but declined. Tissot, mentioned earlier, and Legros came within this category – successful and fashionable artists with much to lose and nothing to gain from the enterprise. But more interesting refusals were those of Corot, Daubigny and even Courbet. In Corot's case, there was definite disapproval. When Antoine Guillemet declined participation, Corot wrote, 'My dear Antoine you have done very well to escape from that gang'. Courbet was currently in exile in Switzerland for his 'subversive' political activity during the Commune, but might well have had other reasons not to participate. The most significant refusal, as we saw in Part 1, was Manet's.

The exhibition opened in 1874 on April 15, and ran for a month. 165 works were included. By our standards this makes it a major show. But by contemporary Salon standards it was very small indeed. The Salon of that year included approximately 4,000 works, and Zola calculated that it was visited by a staggering 400,000 people. Perhaps 3,500 visited the 'First Impressionist Exhibition'. Of the latter, Zola tells us, the majority came to laugh. So for every person who visited the *Société* exhibition, a hundred or more visited the Salon. Even allowing for exaggeration and for griping on Zola's part, it remains clear that the first exhibition was what avant-garde exhibitions seem to have remained, on the whole, throughout the modern period: exclusive events patronized by a few people with a serious interest in or developed understanding of art. Other factors influencing the nature and number of the visitors may have been, for example, the lack of publicity for unfamiliar names and venues, in contrast to the familiar tradition of the Salon exhibitions. Thus the size and nature of the attendance should be taken into account in assessing the criticisms of the exhibition, their concerns and intended readership.

To understand quite what the critics were reacting to, it will help to know what the various artists actually showed.

Monet	12 works	(7 oils and 5 pastels)
Degas	10	(oils, pastels, drawings of races, dancers and laundresses)
Morisot	9	(oils, watercolours, pastels)
Renoir	7	(including 1 pastel)
Pissarro	5	(all landscapes)
Sisley	5	(all landscapes)
Guillaumin	3	(all landscapes)
Cézanne	3	(*A Modern Olympia, Maison du Pendu,* and one other)

The other 111 works were submitted by that host of 'lesser names' we have mentioned. But that should make us pause. How many of these others were there? There were twenty-two; which entails that on average, each of these others exhibited no less than five works. The average for our group above is only between six and seven, and that figure is only higher because of the inclusion of so many Monets, Degas and Morisots. Of these three, only Monet was predominantly a 'landscape' Impressionist. It is a significant question, then, why the landscapes of the Impressionists attracted so much of what critical attention the exhibition received, and why Degas was *not* singled out for special comment, as Berthe Morisot was to some extent, especially given his pre-eminent role in the organization of the exhibition.

It cannot be over-emphasized how different the exhibition might have looked had it included shall we say, twelve Manets, ten Courbets and nine Corots. Would Degas and Morisot have been assimilated into a 'Naturalist' group with Manet and perhaps Courbet? How startling would Monet, Renoir, Pissarro and Sisley have looked alongside Corot? These are not rhetorical questions. I mention them to emphasize the fact that the First Impressionist Exhibition did *not* portray accurately the context in which those artists who interest us necessarily *wished* to be seen.

Contemporary critical reactions

Opinions differ as to how well the show was received. And of course this is not a simple factual question anyway. What one historian may see as essentially favourable may sometimes be seen as hostile by another, and critics frequently put their points over in guarded, elliptical and carefully balanced (though sometimes carelessly unbalanced) ways. For example, as we have seen, Louis Leroy's famous *Satiric Review of the First Impressionist Exhibition* (*Supplementary Documents*, II.2) is written as a dialogue between himself and the outraged (fictional) academician M. Vincent. Doubtless Vincent's views were typical of many visitors to the exhibition, yet as John House points out (Radiovision programme 5), the voice of Leroy himself makes some not unsympathetic or unperceptive points.

Two things are certain; there *were* hostile criticisms and those so criticized took these to heart. Three years after the event, a critic called F. O'Squarre wrote, 'Public conscience was indignant. This was awful, stupid, dirty; this had no common sense' (quoted in Rewald, page 328). Rewald also quotes a contemporary review, dated 17 April, in which E. d'Hervilly shows what some critics felt to be an appropriate reaction to the 'worst excesses' of the show:

> Shall we speak of M. Cézanne? Of all known juries, none ever imagined, even in a dream, the possibility of accepting any work by this painter who used to present himself at the Salon carrying his canvases on his back like Jesus his cross. A too exclusive love of yellow has up to now compromised the future of M. Cézanne.

Note the pattern of this comment; Cézanne's face doesn't fit, something needs to be mentioned as an excuse for keeping him out and anything will do. Doubtless there were many other objections to Cézanne; but d'Hervilly seems too embarrassed to mention them.

As to how the criticisms felt to Pissarro, in May he wrote to Duret 'The critics are devouring us and accusing us of not studying'. And some years later he wrote to a friend, 'What I have suffered is beyond words. What I suffer at the actual moment is terrible, much more than when I was young, full of enthusiasm and ardour, convinced as I now am of being lost for the future'. In fact however, there *were* sympathetic reviews, if sometimes guardedly so. John House points out that of the ten to have been traced, 'six essentially supported the artists'. Sylvestre and Castagnary are important. But before looking at them in detail, let's set out the principal questions we should be trying to answer when we read them;

1   How much of the criticism was devoted to technical issues, and which were they?

2   How much was written about subject matter and its mode of depiction, and what was said?

3   Which artists attracted attention and how were they characteristically grouped together? Who was ignored?

and for the purposes of this block we should also ask,

4   What did the critics say about Degas' contribution to this exhibition?

Realistically, we are not going to find the complete answers to these questions until more work has been done tracing the actual reviews. But we can still say something worthwhile in answer. One review in particular has always been remembered as *the* critical review, and has correspondingly had a large influence on our *image* of how the exhibition was received. This is Leroy's *Satiric Review* (*Supplementary Documents* II.2).

► Read this now, bearing in mind the above questions and remembering that Pissarro's *Hoar Frost* (**Col. pl. II.23**) and Monet's *Boulevard des Capucines* (**Col. pl.II.4**) are illustrated with this block. ◄

▷ It is interesting to note whom Leroy mentions in his review. Monet, Renoir, Pissarro and Sisley all come in for (dishonourable) mention. But they are not alone. Morisot and Cézanne are also mentioned and taken to task, Degas too and his school friend, the amateur Rouart. (Ottin and Lépine are mentioned in passing as 'normal', in contrast.) 'The group' does not yet exist for Leroy. Interestingly too, Leroy *does* ascribe influence to Corot (as you have seen) and mentions Manet. But, and this is important, the mention of Manet is little more than that. He is not credited with any unhealthy influence as Corot is. Can we guess why? I suggest that Leroy would have regarded Manet as just another of these experimenters, whose absence from the exhibition was perhaps something to be grateful for. In other words, it may not have crossed his mind to ask whether Manet was 'important' enough to be credited with *influence*. This would tie in with our observations in Part 1, to the effect that landscape was a genre in which there was an already established tradition of technical experiment. Perhaps that in turn contributes to our understanding of why the landscape painters were picked out as a group of particular significance. Perhaps landscape was the only area in which radical modes of painting could at least be seen by Leroy for what they were. Indeed, Leroy has nothing to say of the innovator Degas except this: '*The Laundress,* so badly laundered, of M. Degas drove [M. Vincent] to cries of [ironic and facetious] admiration.' He seems almost literally lost for words in front of a novel form of figure painting of the kind which might display Manet's influence. Of a portrait by Morisot, he can only comment on the sketchiness of the painting of the fingers.

    As to the actual content of Leroy's criticisms, this has almost entirely to do with the question of finish; one or two concern colour. There are no comments of any other kind. ◁

Leroy was certainly not alone in homing in on these features, nor in being blind to any connection with Manet. Mme Morisot, Berthe's mother, was anxious to know whether Manet had been right in trying to warn her daughter against joining the exhibitors and sent the artist Guichard for his opinion. He wrote:

> When I entered, I became anguished upon seeing the works of your daughter in those pernicious surroundings. I said to myself; 'one doesn't live with impunity among madmen. Manet was right in opposing her participation'. After examining and analysing conscientiously one certainly finds here and there some excellent fragments, but they all have more or less *cross-eyed minds*.
>
> (Quoted in Rewald, page 325)

There is no sense of irony here – no sense that Manet may have been partly responsible himself for the very works of these 'madmen'. And the reference to 'cross-eyed minds' may well be another reference to lack of finish. Less finished works can often have an 'unfocused' look about them. The critic Cardon also complained about both finish and colour:

> Soil three-quarters of a canvas with black and white, rub the rest with yellow, distribute haphazardly some red and blue spots, and you'll obtain an *impression* of spring in front of which the adepts will be carried away by ecstasy.
>
> ('Avant le Salon – L'Exposition des Revoltés', *La Presse,* 29 April 1874)

Indeed colour became, during the 1870s and 1880s, a very emotive issue in critical writing about Impressionism. It was felt by some, for instance, that they used far too much violet (and related colours). (See for instance, Monet's *Boulevard des Capucines* (**Col. pl.II.**4) and Pissarro's *Factory near Pontoise* (**Col. pl.II.**8).) Supposedly scientific evidence was brought forward to 'prove' that 'excessive' optical sensibility to violet was a clinical disorder, and indeed that it went frequently with pathological psychiatric states. Another theory held it to be a consequence of too much *plein air* painting; excessive *plein air* working would stimulate illusions of violet since violet was the complementary of yellow (more or less) and yellow was the colour of sunlight (again, more or less). Of course these theories are more or less barmy.

Manet's connection with the *Société* painters did not go unnoted by everyone, however. Some simply confused Manet's and Monet's names. The critic Clarétie was more perceptive.

> M. Manet is among those who maintain that in painting one can and ought to be satisfied with the *impression*. We have seen an exhibition by these *impressionalists* [sic] on the boulevard des Capucines, at Nadar's. M. Monet – a more uncompromising Manet – Pissarro, Mlle Morisot, etc. appear to have declared war on beauty.
>
> (Clarétie; *L'art et les artistes français contemporains,* 1875)

What is interesting here is the emphasis on what Degas' 'realist' friends took to be only a secondary characteristic of their work. The 'Impressionist' technique matters at least partly because it is peculiarly suited (in their opinion) to capturing the essence of modern subject matter.

Interestingly, it is to one of the more sympathetic of the critics, quoted earlier, that we have to turn in order to find a discussion of subject matter.

> A blond light floods [their works] and everything in them is gaiety, clarity, spring festival, golden evenings or blooming apple trees.
>
> (Armand Silvestre, *L'Opinion Nationale,* 22 April 1874)

Gushing as this is, and somewhat selective too (how well would it fit Pissarro's *Coach at Louveciennes* or *Factory near Pontoise* or Monet's *Boulevard des Capucines?*) at least the pictures are more for Silvestre than merely failed exercises in style. Unlike, say, Leroy, he has not simply bundled all the work under the one heading 'landscape', but has stopped to ask 'What *kind* of landscape do we have here?'. He is dimly aware of some purpose to it all; aware that different places have a different significance – that a picture of an orchard will not express the same 'meaning' as a picture of an alpine crag, or a view of the Seine with barges.

▶ There is one other reviewer of the first exhibition whose views are particularly illuminating both historically and critically – the 'realist' Castagnary. Please read the extract from his review of 29 April in *Le Siècle* printed in the *Supplementary Documents*, II.3.

What strikes you as the most important point to note in these extracts? The question is difficult, because Castagnary has so much to say that is worth taking note of. ◀

▷ I hope you might have noticed, first, both that Castagnary shares the group's antipathy to the Salon and that he includes Morisot with 'those four young men'. His comment that their work is 'lively, sharp, light' echoes Sylvestre's perception. And he speaks sympathetically of what Clarétie so disliked – their interest in first impressions. But none of these are the most important of his points. His key idea is that 'a school lives on ideas and not on material means, distinguishing itself by its doctrines and not by a technique of execution'. For it's in the light of this idea that he describes and assesses the group's achievement and their probable future.

There is in this statement an implicit rebuke to those critics, who, like Leroy, concerned themselves with questions of technique alone: they must be missing the point. Yet what is the point of these paintings? Castagnary seems to me to be denying that there is *any* specially new 'point' to these pictures; 'to a large extent . . . the forms of art remain unchanged'. What I suspect this means is that genres and principles of composition have *not* been challenged. Indeed Castagnary seems to see in the works of the Impressionists only a new way of achieving well-established aims. But, as we have seen, he had long championed realism in some form or another and what would have struck him as nothing especially new might not have struck a more conservative critic in the same way. In fact it can be argued that he writes from a viewpoint that is already implicitly 'naturalistic' when he says, 'The strongest among them . . . will have recognized that while there are subjects which lend themselves to a rapid "impression", . . . there are others . . . that demand a more precise impression'. What this suggests is that technique should be adapted to the specific requirements of different types of subject, and that the 'modernism' of the Impressionists was perhaps not what was at issue for Castagnary. But from a historian's point of view, Castagnary's review is of value for the light it sheds on both the roots of Modernist criticism of the Impressionists and on the nature of the criticism of Degas. ◁

Modernists have not all shared the same perceptions of Impressionism. While there are those who applaud those Impressionist innovations which they have seen as opening the door to flatness, decorativeness, abstraction and autonomy, there have been others such as Fry who decried what they saw as a passive enslavement to the dictates of the eye, to the demands of mechanical, quasi-photographic representation. Curiously, both views are prefigured in this review of Castagnary's and yet he writes with very similar perceptions and preoccupations to those of any pre-Modernist critic. He *is* concerned with subject matter and ideas, and with questions about representation. On the one hand he pre-echoes Modernist denigrators of the Impressionists when he writes, 'Once the impression is captured, they declare their role terminated'. The force of this sentence is not clear, but it could be taken as suggesting that there is *nothing much to the job* of capturing impressions; as though no insight and even little skill were involved. On the other hand, he seems almost prescient about 'where it will all end'.

You should have been alerted by the use, in the extract, of the word 'pretext'. When Castagnary warns against 'nature becoming a pretext for dreams', you should stop and ask whether he is not saying much the same as the Modernists when they talk of subjects becoming, in Manet for instance, pretexts for 'pure painting'. I think he does mean very much the same. Nature is here implicitly the subject. As for dreams, what he means is the kind of paintings that have departed sufficiently from what we conventionally think of as representations (i.e. pictures involving the production of a likeness of the thing represented), to make it effectively impossible to criticize them in terms of their degree of correspondence to some feature of the actual world. The difference here between Castagnary and some 'pro-Impressionist' Modernists is that they tend to approve of just what he warns against.

What do we learn, then, from looking at criticisms of the first Impressionist exhibition which can give us some bearings for examining contemporary critical writings about Degas? First, we must notice the imbalance between criticisms of technique – of colour, and in particular finish and detail – and on the other hand discussions of subject matter. Even Castagnary neglected the latter. Was Degas treated in this same manner? If so, why: if not, why not? Secondly, we have seen that while Monet, Pissarro, Sisley and Renoir were not immediately selected as the definitive core group, *landscape* was nevertheless a predominant concern of the critics, and one which seems rarely to have been discussed without mention of these four among others. Are these two tendencies – emphasis on landscape and on techniques – linked in any way? And how would we expect Degas to be treated if they *are* linked?

I suspect these tendencies are in fact linked. As we saw in Part 1, 'pure' landscape as such was not among the higher genres for connoisseurs of Salon painting. Were one to set about criticizing landscape, technique, rather than subject, would be the obvious point to home in on. The more difficult question is why the landscapes attracted so disproportionate a share of the attention in the first place. It is tempting to suggest that landscape painting was simply the one place where technical innovation could be seen in the exhibition. But this is not actually true. As you saw in the Leroy review, while Degas' own work was technically unusual, it horrified 'M. Vincent' no less than did the work of the landscape painters.

I have an answer to suggest here. It will help us to put the question on one side for a moment though to consider another critic, Edmond Duranty, writing two years later (1876) about the *second* 'Impressionist exhibition'. Duranty is of particular interest with respect to Degas, but he also sheds light on the question why landscape was so important a theme in reviews of the first exhibition, by virtue of the fact that he *doesn't* talk exclusively about landscape but *does* mention subject matter and modes of depiction.

Duranty was a particular friend of Degas, though he knew well the other major Impressionists. It is often suggested that Duranty really only had sympathy – perhaps only understanding – for Degas and not for the others. It's certainly true that he was not unqualified in his enthusiasm for the landscape painters, and that they were unhappy with the rather guarded review that Duranty gave them; they felt it was disappointing coming from a supposed ally and a former frequenter of the Café Guerbois. This review is often treated as though it were really a covert manifesto for Degas alone. I doubt this. While you read these extracts, ask yourself which of Duranty's points refer principally to Degas and which have a wider significance, embracing the work both of Degas and of the other Impressionists.

▶ Now read the extracts from 'The New Painting; Concerning the Group of Artists Exhibiting at the Durand-Ruel Galleries', which you will find in the *Supplementary Documents*, II.4. ◀

▷ Obviously, what Duranty has to say about drawing and composition (new viewpoints) has a particular relevance to the work of Degas. But, of course, there is also a quite penetrating section on colour, which certainly refers to the landscape painters, rather than to Degas. Criticism was catching up. Less obviously but more importantly, there are points he makes about coherence in the mode of depiction, which are contained in the two paragraphs beginning 'For the observer, there is a whole logic . . . ' (para. 16) and ending '. . . extracts from ready-made painting . . .'. The importance of this short passage is that it applies equally well *both* to the work of Degas *and* to the landscapes of the Impressionists. Now in this idea I think we find the basis of an answer to Castagnary's complaint, that the new painters were promulgating a mere technique, whereas what was needed to make a new school of painting were new *ideas*. And the new idea in question seems to be one which offers an alternative explanation of Impressionism to the Modernist line; the idea that a realistic or a naturalistic art should try to recreate the precise physical characteristics of a scene — that it is not enough for it just to depict 'everyday' subject-matter and to use tricks to give it the look of being real. Naturalistic painting should attempt to show how the scene *really looks* rather than to make the scene *look real*. That surely is what Duranty is trying to say when he talks of the way one would lose 'homogeneity, accord, truthfulness, the impression', in different conditions. (And when he objects, 'This, however, is what is done every day by painters who do not deign to observe . . .' he certainly has in mind the practices of those who painted their figures under quite different light conditions from those which illuminate their landscape.)

This idea of Duranty's is also reflected when he writes, 'The basement with a ray of light coming through a narrow air hole — such was the governing idea of the Romantic artist', and again, 'It was necessary to make the painter leave his sky-lighted cell, . . . to bring him out among men, into the world'. These are clear allusions to the actual architectural design of painters' studios, on the one hand, and to the practice of 'plein-air' painting on the other.

Well nearly so. As I said just now, these ideas of Duranty's apply to Degas as well, and we know that, in a sense, Degas was a studio artist. He never produced 'plein-air' painting (or very rarely). Nonetheless, his reliance on sketches and studies (such as those rapid impressions which Baudelaire so much admired in Constantin Guys' work), meets Duranty's analysis just as well as true 'plein-air' painting does. Back in his studio, Degas would try his best not quite to recreate the real look of any particular scene, but to create precisely the sense of coherence and harmony of light and detail which Duranty talks of. Degas did not paint any one scene as it would have really looked — most of his scenes are constructs, composites of elements from real life. (Drawings exist, for instance, which show one and the same model three or four times over in different poses.) But nor was he concerned to make his pictures *look real* (i.e. finished and absolute) in the sense that Courbet was. It is as though he was seeking the same cohesion and descriptive accuracy that the Impressionists achieved (though most of his scenes are interiors), but without painting direct from the motif itself. And if he was not working direct from life, nor was he giving a faithful reproduction of the artificial conditions of light, composition, posture of models or viewpoint that would obtain in his studio.

It's no accident that Duranty several times mentions the relationship of the group to tradition, and represents them as being in a continual dialogue with tradition. However, when he speaks of some simply transforming tradition while others radically throw over the old techniques, we can be sure that his 'radical of radicals' is Degas; which suggests that he sees the Impressionists themselves as very firmly rooted in traditions which they simply transform. Thus it becomes appropriate to look carefully at their subject-matter as well; '. . . the trembling of leaves, the shivering of water, and the vibration of air inundated with light and . . . the soft ambiance of a grey day . . .' But of course Degas' subjects — or potential subjects — are equally worthy of mention as novel; 'the railway, the linen-drapers shop, the scaffoldings of construction, the lines of gas lights, the boulevard benches with the newspaper stands . . .'

▶ You should now read the text by Huysmans in the Reader (Text 8), paying particular attention to the two paragraphs from 'It is difficult to convey in writing . . . (page 47) to '. . . deemed impossible to represent in painting.' ◀

In these two reviews we have, I think, a major clue as to why critics of the *first* exhibition homed in on the landscape paintings so exclusively and dealt with them in terms of technique. However objectionable Degas' themes and modes of depiction of those themes may have been to contemporary critics, there was nonetheless a *literary* quality about both which made them accessible to the ordinary art lover of 1874–6 and later. Look for instance at *Interior* (*The Rape*, **Pl. II.63**). This is said to depict a scene from Zola's novel, *Thérèse Raquin,* a gruesome story which still had the power to shock when serialized by BBC Television in 1979. Now there are many naturalistic touches to this picture – the poses, the glow of the light, the careful rendering of the wallpaper and so on. But these are not at the forefront of our attention. With the landscapes, all is different. It is difficult actually to see anything as transient and seemingly trivial as the rustling of leaves or the shivering of water as the *subject* of a painting, and impossible to see a story in such things. We can see now that to find themselves confronted with pictures which both made technical innovations and yet were also 'meaningless' from the point of view of literary or narrative interpretation must have been disorienting to critics of the day, who had no well-formed vocabulary to describe and explain their appearance. If the works lack 'meaning' why go through the dangerous passes of technical innovation to achieve them? Accordingly, the landscape works were not seen as innovative, but merely as 'daubs'. And I suggest that if Degas, and Morisot in her figure work, were not so much the centre of attention, it is because it was paradoxically easiest to fit them within a rather literary frame of expectations. Yes, they were novel, innovative and an unwelcome challenge (to some). Huysmans credits Degas with 'translating effects hitherto misunderstood or deemed impossible to represent in painting'. But his works were not seen as meaningless, and therefore not as a direct affront to accepted criteria of competence. Thus they were also less urgently interesting. (For a further example of a contemporary critic's response to Degas' scenes and modes of depiction, read Fénéon, *Supplementary Documents,* III.2.)

The Impressionists and Degas in the Modernist critical tradition

If you look again at the opening two paragraphs of this block you may now understand more clearly why such issues were raised at the outset. It often seems as if criticism of painting in the modern period has concentrated on matters of technique, and that assessments of technical competence and invention are what decide above all how an artist's work is understood and esteemed. Yet what the preceding discussion suggests – and Tim Clark makes a similar point in his article on 'Manet's *Olympia* in 1865' (Reader, Text 40) – is that how a critic regards and assesses technique may well merely follow from a judgement *already made* on the basis of subject matter. Where that judgement is favourable (as it may be where the critic can see the subject matter as properly secured by conventions and principles of decorum) discussion of technique will tend to emphasize how well it serves to express the subject. But where it is *unfavourable* (as in the case of Manet's *Olympia* and the landscapes of the Impressionists) a concentration on discussion of technique and of technical incompetence may really serve to *cover up* the critic's discomfort at the nature of the subject and at the inadequacy of his or her own descriptive, interpretative and explanatory vocabulary. If the critic cannot understand *what* is represented and expressed, he or she will want to assume that the fault lies with the *means* of expression. Our own failures to understand are all too often attributed to the failure of others properly to 'communicate'.

For the Modernist, such symptoms of painting's capacity to evade linguistic description are just what will be looked for as means to identify critical moments in the development of the art.

According to the view of the development of modern painting which Greenberg advances in 'Modernist Painting' (Reader, Text 1), the very avoidance of 'literary' or story-telling content in Impressionism, combined with an emphasis upon the expressive potential of the flat painted surface itself, is what gives Impressionist painting its distinctive position in modern art history. According to his terms, these are just the qualities which are likely to have made Impressionism 'urgently interesting'. We can now perhaps see more easily why Modernists should need either to 'modernize' Degas – i.e. to regard him as a kind of proto-abstract artist *despite* his subjects – or to treat him as a possibly interesting figure outside the mainstream.

► There are various arguments against such a treatment of the art we have been considering in this block. Can you think of some? (This is not an easy exercise.) ◄

▷ 1   We could point out – as we tried to do in Part 1 – that a concern for the realistic nature of certain types of subjects underlies the typical works of the Impressionists in the late 1860s and the 1870s (and of Pissarro beyond that date), and therefore that Degas cannot be prised apart from them on those grounds. Whatever the Modernist may take to be the visible pictorial *effects* of Impressionist painting, the techniques they used can still be seen as means to establish reference to and illusion of a three-dimensional world. To see these paintings as comparatively flat is retrospectively to apply a frame of reference irrelevant to what the artists were actually doing or trying to do. This doesn't definitely contradict what the Modernist says, since he or she can still say that *he* or *she* sees the paintings as (comparatively) flat. It implies, rather, that the price paid for singling out this aspect is to lose sight of others which may be equally, or more, important or interesting.

2   We could offer a similar argument against the view of Degas' works as 'abstract'. It may help to extend the scope of modern forms of criticism, but it doesn't accord very well with what Degas seems to have been trying to do. Such assessments as those of Samuel Lane Faison, Sandra Orienti and John Rewald, quoted at the outset of Part 2, seem to suggest that what was importantly particular for Degas in the dancers and laundresses and nudes he drew and painted was simply the qualities of the poses they presented, and the pictorial arrangements of colour and form he could derive from them. But it is clear from contemporary reactions, such as Edmond de Goncourt's, that his audience understood very well that Degas' choice of particular *types* of women, represented in particular circumstances, was in itself significant. Huysmans, for instance, is concerned both to catalogue Degas' subjects and to express his disappointment at the lack of engagement with modern subjects on the part of the 'landscape artists'. Eunice Lipton provides strong evidence to support the view that Degas' subjects were very much more than 'pretexts' for the 'representation of colour and form'.

3   We could try to argue against the view that Degas' place is outside the mainstream of modern development. To do this would be to engage with a much wider argument. We would have to challenge the prevailing interpretation of subsequent art history, and the account offered by such writers as Greenberg of an inexorable tendency towards autonomy for the expressive decorated surface, and thus towards

abstraction. Such a challenge would require that we pick out instead those aspects of subsequent modern art history which reveal a persistent concern with what Degas saw as 'realism': that attempt to capture the changing character of modern life and to represent it in some typical and vivid moment which Huysmans and others so clearly admired in Degas' work. We shall see in Block XII that the work of Degas was certainly important for a group of English artists in the early twentieth century who seem to have had similar concerns. But perhaps what we should attempt is not to rewrite art history so that different artists emerge as the 'major figures', or different concerns as the 'major concerns'. We should rather be alert to the deficiencies and closures of *any* single linear account of the development of modern art. ◁

The brief discussion of autonomy and 'realism' at the close of Section 5 of the *Introduction* may help to explain why (page 23). What this suggests, in relation to Degas, is that if we are to make sense of his activity we need to consider the tension between two dialectical conditions: on the one hand, the demands of realistic description – the requirement of fidelity to what was specific in the circumstances of actual people in the world he observed; and on the other, the demands of picture-making – the manipulation of materials and formal motifs on the flat surface of the paper or canvas. Within the French art world of the 1860s–1880s, each of these demands was conceived and discussed within a lively critical and professional discourse by people with different interests and commitments, and with different ideas about how the two demands should be reconciled. The review by Huysmans, for instance, shows that he was sensitive both to the 'realism' of Degas' subjects ('What truth! What life!'), and to the modernism of his techniques ('What a new way of applying the rules of optical mixing'). The very liveliness of this discourse helps to account for the variety of French art in the later nineteenth century. To draw out any one line through the art of the period is to risk losing sight of this variety.

As regards the subsequent fortunes of Impressionism in the Modernist critical tradition, we need to isolate two different strands, the first within English criticism *c.* 1900–20, the second within American criticism since the Second World War. It is important to remember that the most influential interpretations of the place of Impressionism in modern art history as a whole have been made by critics with strong commitments to specific subsequent developments; in the former case to what became known as 'Post-Impressionism'; and in the latter to American 'Abstract Expressionism'.

In 1910, in calling the first of his two major exhibitions of recent European art 'Manet and the Post-Impressionists' (and in excluding the Impressionists from his survey), Roger Fry was allying himself clearly with that critique of naturalism, and of the Impressionists as too slavishly bound by actual appearances, which had gained strength in Europe since the 1880s. He and Clive Bell found the work of the Impressionists both too informal – i.e. too much lacking in what Bell called 'significant form'– and too closely linked to theories about colour and light, to serve as means to that expression of feeling and emotion which they saw as the primary function of art. As Fry wrote in 'Retrospect' in 1920, 'After a brief period during which I was interested in the new possibilities opened up by the more scientific evaluation of colour which the Impressionists practised, I came to feel more and more the absence in their work of structural design'.

Cézanne, and to a lesser extent the other 'Post-Impressionists', were seen as having reintroduced the 'plastic values' found in the art of the great ages and subdued by the Impressionist 'dissolution of form'. Bell dismissed Monet's late works as 'polychromatic charts of desolating dullness' (*Art* 1914). Renoir's late work, on the other hand, was celebrated by both Fry and Bell, as a reaffirmation, as Bell put it, of 'What every artist knows, that art is the creation and not the imitation of form'. Bell saw the designation of Renoir as an Impressionist as 'an honour he neither desires nor deserves', and in 1919, after the death of Cézanne, could write of him as 'the greatest painter alive'. Such assessments of Renoir's later work are echoed by Hamilton, as you may have noted.

Where Degas' work was discussed by Fry and Bell, it tended to be distinguished from the Impressionists much as the later work of Renoir was. Fry, in his 'Retrospect', wrote 'I was always able to admit the greatness of Degas . . .', but he seems to have felt no need to explain or justify this assessment. Perhaps, as we have suggested, this was precisely because Degas' work was not seen as presenting any problems for the prevailing and secure means of appreciation. Pissarro, where he figures at all in the English criticism of this period, tends to be credited principally with the role of mentor to Cézanne.

In the later, 'American' phase of Modernist criticism, Impressionism was reintroduced as the transitional stage between Manet and Post-Impressionism, and the 'informality' which had disappointed Fry was revalued. The 'all-over', broken paintwork of the typical Impressionist picture was now re-established as a necessary step in that recognition of the picture surface as a 'physical entity' which Greenberg saw as characterizing the development of Modernist painting. This revaluation was no doubt encouraged by the work of the art-historian John Rewald. His massive *History of Impressionism* was completed during the Second World War and was first published by the Museum of Modern Art in New York in 1946. (We shall have cause further to examine the operations of this powerful institution in later blocks.) Ten years later this study was followed by the same author's *Post-Impressionism*, in matching format. A high proportion of the numerous illustrations in both books were of works in American collections. Between 1938 and 1948 Rewald also published books on Gauguin, Seurat, Cézanne, Bonnard, Degas' sculpture and Renoir's drawings, and edited the letters of Cézanne, Gauguin and Pissarro. Such studies must have done much to emphasize the complex nature of the relations between those earlier separated into 'Impressionists' and 'Post-Impressionists'. They must also have encouraged interested American writers and collectors to see French art of the later nineteenth century as properly incorporated into the cultural heritage (and property) of American Modernism. (In 1885 Durand-Ruel, in a somewhat desperate search for new markets, had accepted an invitation from the American Art Association to organize a substantial exhibition in New York the following year. Monet seems to have seen this venture as positively inhibiting to his own attempts to establish a place in art history. Durand-Ruel, however, was pleasantly surprised by the interest shown in his wares.)

The flavour of more recent American Modernist interest in the work of the Impressionists can be sampled in one (admittedly somewhat extreme) quotation.

> Impressionism, more than any prior movement in the history of art, rejects functional analysis out of hand. Its iconology is uninteresting, its sociohistorical role unimportant. The greatness and the depth of Impressionist painting lies, so to speak on its surface . . .

(Kermit Champa, *Studies in Early Impressionism*, 1973)

References and further reading

Those marked with an asterisk are recommended for further reading.

Blanche, Jacques Émile, *De David à Degas*, Paris, 1919.

*Brettall, Richard, 'Camille Pissarro – A Revision' in *Camille Pissarro 1830–1903*, exhibition catalogue, Arts Council of Great Britain and the Museum of Fine Arts, Boston, 1980.

Buerger, Janet F., 'Degas' Solarized and Negative Photographs: A Look at Unorthodox Classicism', *Image*, Vol. 2, 1978.

Champa, Kermit, *Studies in Early Impressionism*, Yale University Press, 1974.

Clark, Timothy J., 'Preliminaries to a Possible Treatment of *Olympia* in 1865', *Screen*, Spring 1980, Volume 21, Number 1, pages 18–51. (Edited reprint in the Reader.)

Dunlop, Ian, *Degas*, Thames and Hudson, 1979.

*Greenberg, Clement, 'Cézanne' (1951), reprinted in *Art and Culture*, Thames and Hudson, 1973. (First published 1961.)

*Greenberg, Clement, 'On the Role of Nature in Modernist Painting' (1949), reprinted in *Art and Culture*, Thames and Hudson, 1973. (First published 1961.)

Guérin, Marcel, (ed.) *Lettres de Degas*, Paris, 1945 (1st edn, 1931).

Holt, Elizabeth G., *A Documentary History of Art*, Vol. III, Doubleday, 1966.

Janis, Eugenia P., *Degas Monotypes*, Garland, 1968.

Lipton, Eunice, 'The Laundress in Late Nineteenth-century French Culture: Imagery. Ideology and Edgar Degas', *Art History*, Vol. 3, No. 3, Sept. 1980, pp. 295–313. (Edited reprint in the Reader.)

Nochlin, Linda, *Realism*, Penguin Books, 1971.

*Nochlin, Linda, *Realism and Tradition in Art 1848–1900 — Sources and Documents*, Prentice Hall, 1966.

Orienti, Sandra, *Degas: the life and work of the artist*, Thames and Hudson, 1969. Translated by Rosalind Hawkes.

Pool, Phoebe, *Impressionism*, Thames and Hudson, 1967.

*Reff, Theodore, *The Notebooks of Edgar Degas*, 2 vols, Clarendon Press, 1976.

*Reff, Theodore, *Degas: The Artist's Mind*, Thames and Hudson, 1976.

*Rewald, John, *The History of Impressionism*, The Museum of Modern Art, New York, 1961. (First published in 1946; fourth edition published in England by Secker and Warburg, 1973, revised 1980.)

Rewald, John, ' "Un article inédit" sur Paul Cézanne, 1870.' *Arts*, Paris, July 21–27, 1954.

*Rewald, John, *Post-Impressionism, from Van Gogh to Gauguin*, Secker and Warburg, 1978. (First published by The Museum of Modern Art, 1956.)

Schapiro, Meyer, 'The Nature of Abstract Art', reprinted in Meyer Schapiro, *Modern Art. 19th and 20th Centuries*, Chatto and Windus, 1978. (First published in *Marxist Quarterly*, Vol. I, Number 1, 1937.) (Reprinted in *Supplementary Documents* VII.5.)

Venturi, Lionello, 'Impressionism', *Encyclopedia of Modern Art*, Vol VII, Col. 825–6, 1963.

Appendix List of participants in Impressionist group exhibitions

	1874	1876	1877	1879	1880	1881	1882	1886
Astruc	●							
Attendu	●							
Béliard	●	●						
Boudin	●							
Bracquemond, F.	●			●	●			
Bracquemond, Mme				●	●			●
Brandon	●							
Bureau	●							
Caillebotte		●	●	●	●		●	
Cals	●	●	●	●				
Cassatt				●	●	●		●
Cézanne	●		●					
Colin	●							
Cordey			●					
Debras	●							
Degas	●	●	●	●	●	●		●
Desboutin		●						
Forain				●	●	●		
François		●	●					
Gauguin				●	●	●	●	●
Guillaumin	●		●		●	●	●	●
Lamy			●					
Latouche	●							
Lebourg				●	●			
Legros		●						
Lepic	●	●						
Levert	●							
Lépine	●	●	●		●			
Maureau			●					
Meyer	●							
Millet, J. B.		●						
de Molins	●							
Monet	●	●	●	●			●	
Morisot	●	●	●		●	●	●	●
Mulot-Durivage	●							
de Nittis	●							
Ottin, A.	●							
Ottin, L.	●	●						
Piette			●	●				
Pissarro, C.	●	●	●	●	●	●	●	●
Pissarro, L.								●
Raffaëlli					●	●		
Redon								●
Renoir	●	●	●				●	
Robert	●							
Rouart	●	●	●	●	●	●		●
Schuffenecker								●
Seurat								●
Signac								●
Sisley	●	●	●				●	
Somm				●				
Tillot		●	●	●		●		●
Vidal					●	●		
Vignon					●	●	●	●
Zandomeneghi				●	●	●		●

After J. Rewald, The History of Impressionism, Secker *and Warburg, 1973, page 591. First published by The Museum of Modern Art, New York, 1946.*